Masses

Part 2

Recent Researches in Music

A-R Editions publishes seven series of critical editions, spanning the history of Western music, American music, and oral traditions.

Recent Researches in the Music of the Middle Ages and Early Renaissance
Charles M. Atkinson, general editor

Recent Researches in the Music of the Renaissance
James Haar, general editor

Recent Researches in the Music of the Baroque Era
Christoph Wolff, general editor

Recent Researches in the Music of the Classical Era
Eugene K. Wolf, general editor

Recent Researches in the Music of the Nineteenth and Early Twentieth Centuries
Rufus Hallmark, general editor

Recent Researches in American Music
John M. Graziano, general editor

Recent Researches in the Oral Traditions of Music
Philip V. Bohlman, general editor

Each edition in *Recent Researches* is devoted to works by a single composer or to a single genre. The content is chosen for its high quality and historical importance, and each edition includes a substantial introduction and critical report. The music is engraved according to the highest standards of production using the proprietary software MusE, owned by Music|Notes.™

For information on establishing a standing order to any of our series, or for editorial guidelines on submitting proposals, please contact:

A-R Editions, Inc.
801 Deming Way
Madison, Wisconsin 53717

800 736-0070 (U.S. book orders)
608 836-9000 (phone)
608 831-8200 (fax)
http://www.areditions.com

RECENT RESEARCHES IN THE MUSIC OF THE MIDDLE AGES AND EARLY RENAISSANCE, 35

Johannes Martini

Masses

Part 2
Masses with Known Polyphonic Models

Edited by Elaine Moohan and Murray Steib

A-R Editions, Inc.
Madison

A-R Editions, Inc., Madison, Wisconsin 53717
© 1999 by A-R Editions, Inc.

All rights reserved. No part of this book may be reproduced or transmitted in any form by any electronic or mechanical means (including photocopying, recording, or information storage and retrieval) without permission in writing from the publisher.

The purchase of this work does not convey the right to perform it in public, nor to make a recording of it for any purpose. Such permission must be obtained in advance from the publisher.

A-R Editions is pleased to support scholars and performers in their use of *Recent Researches* material for study or performance. Subscribers to any of the *Recent Researches* series, as well as patrons of subscribing institutions, are invited to apply for information about our "Copyright Sharing Policy."

Printed in the United States of America

ISBN 0-89579-434-9
ISSN 0362-3572

♾ The paper used in this publication meets the minimum requirements of the American National Standard for Information Sciences—Permanence of Paper for Printed Library Materials, ANSI Z39.48-1984.

Contents

Acknowledgments vi
Missa Cela sans plus 1
Missa Coda di pavon 42
Missa In feuers hitz 73
Missa La Martinella 93
Missa Ma bouche rit 152
  Credo (Alternate Version) 182
Missa Or sus, or sus 190
Missa Nos amis 228
Critical Report 269
  List of Sigla and Abbreviations 269
  Editorial Method 272
  Critical Notes 273
Appendix: Polyphonic Models 285
  Cela sans plus, *Colinet de Lanoy / Johannes Martini* 287
  Der Pfobenschwancz, *Barbingant* 290
  In feuers hitz, *Anonymous* 292
  La Martinella, *Johannes Martini* 294
  Ma bouche rit, *Johannes Okeghem* 298
  Or sus, or sus, *Anonymous* 301
  Nos amys, *A[drien] Basin* 303
  Notes and Texts 304

Acknowledgments

I would like to take this opportunity to thank those who contributed in various ways, and at various stages, to the completion of this edition. To the librarians and library assistants at the libraries central to this study, particularly the staff at the Biblioteca Estense, Modena, for their help during study visits. My thanks to those who offered advice and support as the edition progressed. To Jaap van Benthem, who was always willing to discuss the many problems associated with transcriptions of this nature. To the singers with whom I worked in Glasgow and Manchester, who brought the music alive and patiently allowed me to experiment with text underlay. To my family for their constant support. But my most sincere thanks are extended to David Fallows who directed me towards the Ferrarese manuscripts and whose inspiration remained a guiding force throughout. Finally, I should like to dedicate this edition to Emma who is still discovering the wonders and beauties of this world with a never-diminishing enthusiasm.

Elaine Moohan

I owe a great debt of gratitude to the many people who have helped this edition along at various stages. In particular, I would like to thank Lewis Lockwood, who made available documents from his trips to Italy; Peter Burkholder, who shared his transcriptions of several of the Masses with me; Standley Howell, who read many drafts of the introduction and gave valuable advice; and Stefano Mengozzi, who read every note of the edition and made many trenchant comments about editorial accidentals. The edition is the richer for their insights and help. I would also like to thank the Early Music Study Group at the University of Chicago who sang through several of the Masses and gave me a glimpse of what Martini sounds like. Finally, I would like to thank the late Howard Brown, who first kindled my interest in Martini, and whose guidance, support, and encouragement remain a constant inspiration.

Murray Steib

Missa Cela sans plus

Kyrie

VatS 51, fols. 155ᵛ–165

18
Chri- ste ⟨e- ley- - -
Chri- ste ⟨e- ley-
25
Chri- ste e- ley-
- - - son, Chri- - -
Chri- ste
- - - son, Chri- ste⟩
31
- - - - - son.
- ste⟩ e- - ley- - - son.
e- - ley- - - son.
e- - ley- - - son.

37
Ky- ri- e ⟨e- - ley-
Ky- ri- - e ⟨e- ley- - - son, Ky-
Ky- ri- e ⟨e- ley- - son, Ky- ri-
Ky- ri- e ⟨e- ley- -
44
- son, Ky- ri-
- ri- - e⟩ e-
- - - - - e⟩
-son, Ky- ri- - - e⟩ e- -
51
-e⟩ e- - ley- - - son.
-ley- - - - - - son.
e- ley- - - - son.
- ley- - - - - - son.

Gloria

19
Gra- ti- as a- gi- mus ti- bi pro- pter
glo- ri- fi- ca- mus te. Gra- ti- as a- gi- mus ti- -
Gra- ti- as a- gi- mus ti-
-fi- ca- - mus te. Gra- ti- as a- gi- mus ti-
25
ma- gnam glo- ri- am tu- am. Do-
-bi [pro- pter ma- gnam] Do- - - mi- - ne
-bi [pro- pter ma- gnam]
- bi pro- pter ma- - gnam
31
- mi- ne De- us, Rex cae- le- -
De- us, Rex cae- le- stis, De- us

6

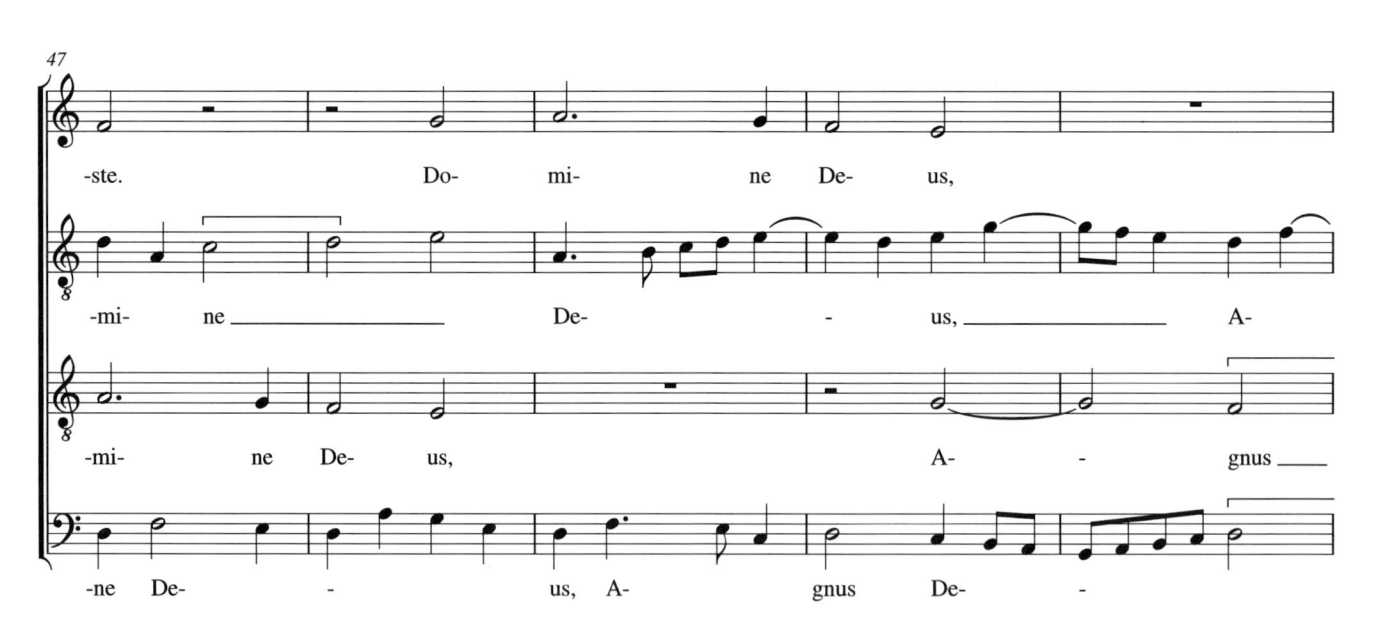

52
A- - gnus De- - i, Fi- li- -
- - gnus De- - i,] Fi- li- -
De- - i, Fi- li- - -
- - - - - i,] Fi-
58
- us Pa- - - tris.
- - us Pa- - - tris.
-us Pa- - - - - tris.
- - li- us Pa- - tris.
64
Qui tol- lis pec- ca- -
Qui tol- lis

-ta _____ mun - di, ____ mi- se-

pec- ca- ta ____ mun- di, _____ mi- se-

-re- re _____ no-

-re- - - - -

-bis. ___ Qui tol- lis ____

Qui tol- lis _____

Qui

-re no- - - - bis. ____

pec- ca- ta mun- di, pec- ca- ta mun- di, tol- lis pec- ca- ta, su- sci- pe su- sci- pe de- su- sci- pe de- ca- ta de- pre- ca- pre- ca- ti- o- nem no- stram. Qui pre- ca- ti- o- nem ti- o- nem no- stram. Qui

104
se- des ad dex- te- - ram Pa- tris,
no- - - stram.
Qui
se- des ad dex- te- ram
109
mi- se- re- re no- - bis.
[Quo- ni- am] tu
se- des ad dex- te- ram
Pa- - tris, mi- se- -
115
tu so-
so- lus San- - ctus, [tu so- -
Pa- tris,
- re- - re no- - - -

11

12

13

Credo

15

27
an- te o- mni- a sae- cu- - la: lu-
na-tum an- te o- mni- a sae- cu- la: De- um de
[De- um de
na-tum an- te o- mni- a sae- cu- la: De- um de De-
32
- men de lu- - mi- ne,
De- o, lu-men de lu- mi- ne,
De- o, lu- men de lu- mi- ne, De-um ve- - rum de De- o
-o, lu- men de lu- mi- ne, De- um ve- rum de De-
37
ge- ni- tum, non fa- ctum,
ge- ni- tum, non fa- ctum, con- - sub- stan-
ve- ro, ge- ni- tum, non
-o ve- ro, ge- ni- tum, non fa- ctum, con-

42
con- sub-stan- ti- - a- - lem Pa- tri, per quem
- ti- a-lem Pa- - tri,] Qui pro-
fa- - ctum, per quem o-
-sub- stan- ti- a- - lem Pa- tri, per quem o- mni- a
46
o-mni- a fa- cta sunt. Qui pro- pter nos ho- - mi- nes,
-pter nos ho- mi- nes, et pro- pter no- stram sa- lu- tem de-
-mni- a fa- cta sunt.] Qui pro- pter nos ho- mi-
fa- cta sunt. Qui pro- pter nos ho- mi- - nes] de-
50
et pro- pter no- stram sa- lu- - tem de-scen-dit de cae- lis.
- scen- dit de- - cae- - lis.
-nes, et pro- pter nos-tram sa- - lu- tem de- scen- dit de cae- lis.
-scen- dit de cae- lis.

55
Et in-
Et in- car- na- tus est
Et in- car- na- tus est
61
-car- na- tus est
de Spi- - ri- tu San- cto,
de
67
de Spi- - ri- tu
⟨de Spi- - ri- - tu
Spi- - ri- tu San- - cto, ⟨de

19

74

Sancto ⟩ ex Ma- ri- a

Sancto ⟩ ex Ma- ri- a

Spi- ri- tu San- cto ⟩ ex Ma- ri- a

81

ex Ma- ri- a Vir- gi-

Vir- gi- ne,

Vir- gi- ne, ⟨ ex Ma- ri-

88

-ne, ⟨ex Ma- ri-

⟨ex Ma- ri a Vir-

-a Vir- gi- ne,⟩

94
- a Vir- - gi- - ne,⟩
- gi- - - - ne,⟩
100
3
et ho- mo fa- ctus
et ho- mo fa- ctus
et ho- mo ⟨fa- ctus est, et ho-
107
est.
est.
- mo⟩ fa- ctus est.

21

136
et re- sur- re- xit ter- ti- a di- e, se-
et re- sur- re- xit ter- ti- a di- e, se- cun-
est, [et
est, et re- - - sur- re- - xit
143
-cun- dum Scri- - ptu- - ras, et a- scen- dit in
- dum Scri- ptu- ras, et a- scen- dit
a- scen- dit in
ter- ti- a di- e,
150
cae- - lum: se- det ad dex- te- - ram Pain cae- lum: [se- det ad dex- te-
cae- lum: se- det ad dex-
Et i- te- rum ven- tu-

157
- tris. Et i- te- - rum ven- - tu- - rus est
-ram Pa- tris. Et i- te- - rum
-te- ram Pa- - - -
- rus est cum glo- ri-
163
cum glo- ri- a, ju- di- ca- re vi- vos
ven- tu- - rus est cum glo- ri- a, ju- di-
- tris. ju- di- ca- - re
- a, ju- - di- ca- re vi- vos et
169
et mor- - tu- os: cu- jus re-
- ca- - re vi- vos cu- - jus re- gni
vi- vos et mor- tu- os:]
mor- - tu- os:

176
-gni non e- rit fi- -
non e- rit fi- -
cu- jus re- gni non e- rit fi-
cu- jus re- gni non e- rit fi- nis.
181
3
-nis. Et ex- spe- cto re- sur- re- cti- o-
-nis.] Et ex- spe- cto
-nis. Et ex- spe- cto
Et ex- spe- cto re- sur-
187
- - - nem mor- tu- o-
re- sur- re- cti- o- nem
re- sur- re- cti- o- nem
- re- cti- - o- nem] et

25

Sanctus

19
- - - - - ctus,⟩
- - - - - -
San- - - - ctus Do-
⟨San- - - ctus, San- -
25
San- - ctus Do- mi-
- ctus, San- - - - ctus Do- mi-
-mi- - nus De- - -
- ctus, San- - ctus⟩ [Do- mi- - - -
31
-nus De- us
- nus De- - us⟩ Sa- - ba- - -
- us Sa- ba-
- nus De- us, De- - - - us

38
Sa- ba- oth.
oth.
pleni sunt tacet
oth.
Sa- ba- oth.]
44
[S]
[CT]
B
Ple- ni
Ple- ni sunt
51
sunt cae- li
cae-
57
et ter-
li et ter-

64
ra
ra
glo-
et
70
ri-
ter-
ra
76
glo-
ri-
a
a,
⟨glo-
ri-
glo-
81
⟨tu-
a,
tu-
a,
tu-
ri-
a,
⟨tu-

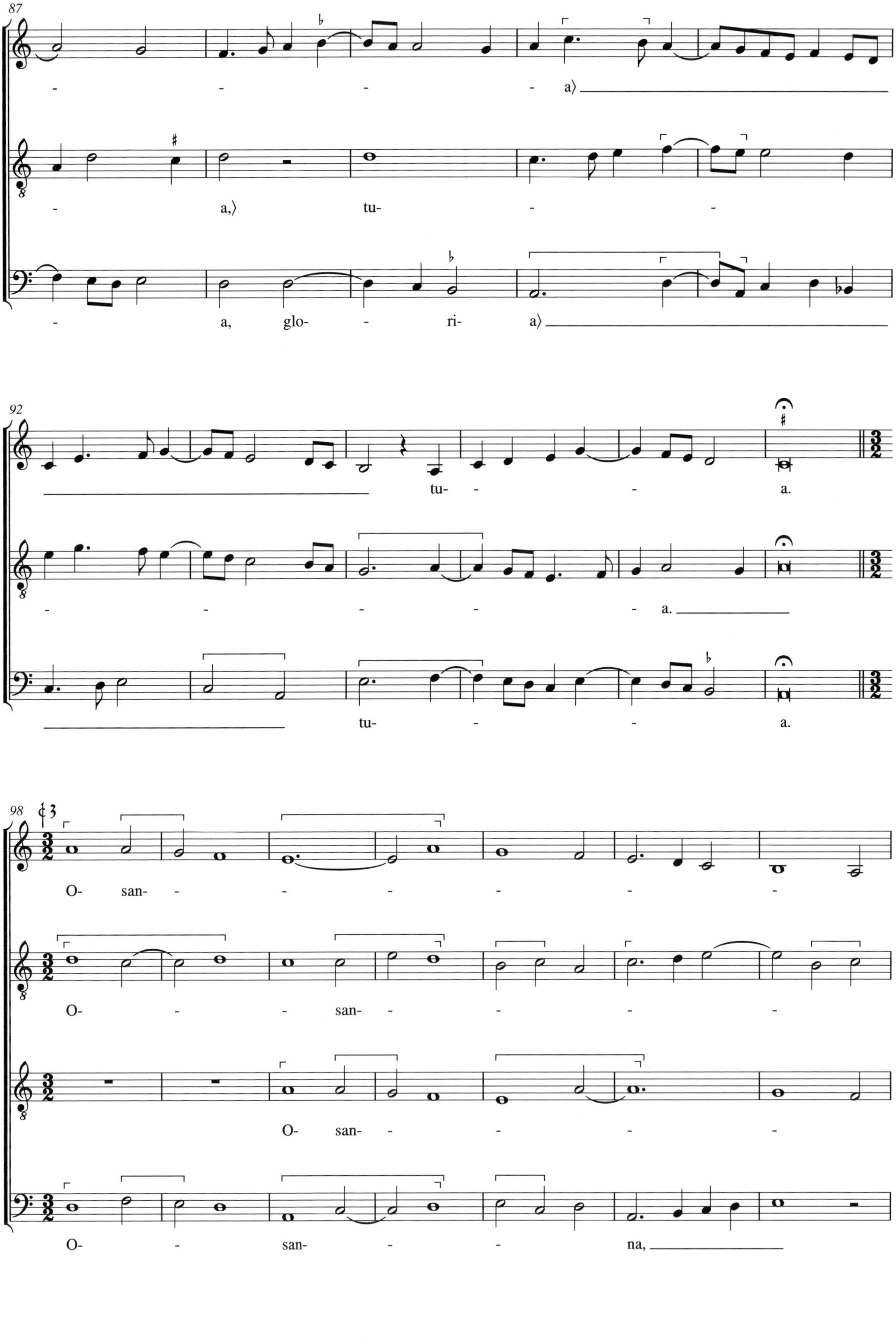
87
- - - - a⟩
- a,⟩ tu- - -
- a, glo- - ri- a⟩
92
tu- - a.
- - - - - a.
tu- - - a.
98
[S]
O- san- - - - - - -
[CT]
O- - - san- - - - -
T
O- san- - - - -
B
O- - san- - - na,

31

126
-cel- - - - sis,⟩
-cel- - sis,⟩ in ex-
in ex- cel-
⟨ex- cel-
132
ex- cel- - sis.
- - - - cel- sis, ⟨ex- cel- sis.⟩
[Benedictus tacet]
Osanna ut supra
- - - - - sis.
- sis,⟩ ex- cel- sis.
139
[S]
Be- - ne- di- - - -
[CT]
Be- - ne- di- -
B

145
- ctus qui ve- -
- - - ctus
150
- - nit in
qui ve- nit, ⟨qui
156
no- mi- - - ne
ve- - -
162
- nit, qui ve-
⟨qui

168
- - nit, qui ve-
ve- nit,⟩ qui
173
- nit⟩ in no- - mi- -
ve- - - - nit
178
Do- mi- - - -
-ne, ⟨in no- - - mi- ne,
183
- - - - ni,
in

35

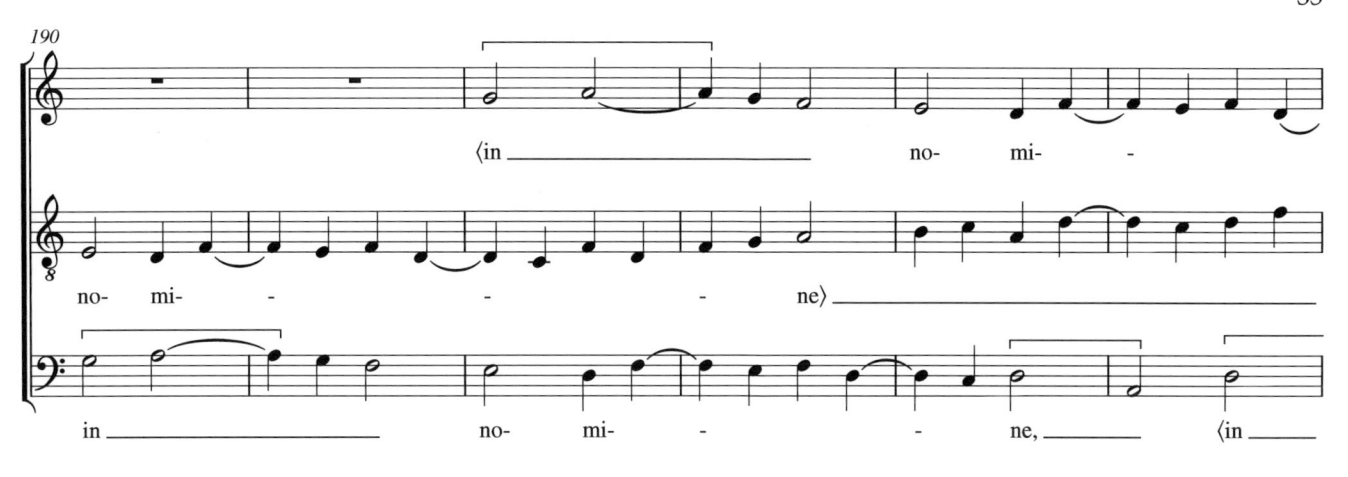

Agnus Dei

17
- - - lis pec- - ca- -
tol- - lis
qui tol- - lis
- - lis⟩
23
- ta
pec- - ca- - - -
pec- ca- - ta mun-
29
mun- di,
- - ta mun- -
pec- ca- - ta mun-
-di, ⟨pec- ca- ta

34
mi- se- re- - -
- - - di,
-di, mi- se- - re- re
mun- di,⟩ mi- se- re- - -
39
- - re no-
mi- se- - re- - re no-
⟨no- - bis,⟩
-re ⟨no- - - - -
44
- - - - bis.
- - - bis.
no- bis.
- bis,⟩ no- bis.

39

65
i,⟩
lis
i,⟩ qui tol- lis
71
qui tol-
pec- ca- ta
pec- ca- ta
77
lis
mun- di, ⟨pec-
mun- di, ⟨pec- ca- ta

83
pec- ca-
-ca- ta mun- - di,⟩
mun- - di,⟩ mi- - se-
88
-ta mun- di, mi- - se- -
mi- se- re- re no- -
- - re- re no-
93
- re- - re no- bis.
Agnus Dei ut supra
- - - bis.
[Agnus Dei ut supra]
[Agnus Dei ut supra]
- - bis.
[Agnus Dei ut supra]

Missa Coda di pavon
Kyrie

ModE M.1.13, no. 11

15
-ste ⟨e- - ley-
-ste ⟨e- ley-
-ste ⟨e- ley- -
-ste ⟨e- ley- -
20
- son, Chri- - - - ste⟩
-son, Chri- ste⟩ e-
-son, Chri- - - ste⟩ e-
- son, Chri- - - - ste⟩
25
e- ley- - son. Ky- ri- e
c
- ley- - son.
-ley- son. Ky-
e- ley- - son.

30
⟨e- ley- - son, Ky- ri- e e-
Ky- ri-
-ri- e ⟨e- - ley son, Ky- ri- e
Ky- - ri- e ⟨e- ley
34
- ley- - son, Ky- ri- e⟩ e-
-e ⟨e- ley- - son, Ky- ri- e⟩ e- ley-
e- - ley- son, Ky- ri- e⟩
son, Ky- ri- -
39
-ley- - - - son.
- - - - son.
e- ley- - - son.
- - e⟩ e- ley- son.

Gloria

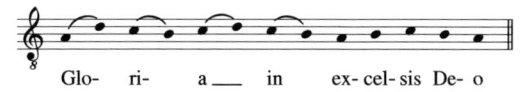

16
te. Gra- ti- as a- gi- mus ti- bi pro-
[te.] Gra- ti- as a- - gi- mus ti- bi
te.]
Gra- ti- as a- gi- mus ti- bi pro-
21
-pter ma- gnam glo- ri- am tu- - am. Do-
[pro- pter ma- gnam glo- ri- - am tu- am. Do- mi-
Do- mi- ne
-pter ma- gnam glo- ri- am tu am.] Do- mi-
26
-mi- ne De- us, Rex cae- le- stis, De- us Pa- ter o-
-ne De- us, Rex cae- le- - stis, De-
De- us, Rex cae- le- stis, De- us Pa- ter
- ne De- us, Rex [cae- le- stis, De- us Pa-

31
-mni- po- tens.
Do- mi- ne Fi- li u- ni- ge-
us Pa- ter]
Do- mi- ne Fi- li u- ni- ge-
[o- mni- po- tens.]
-ter]
Do- mi- ne Fi- li [u- ni- ge-
37
ni- te, Je- su Chri- ste.
-ni- te, [Je- su Chri- ste.]
Je- su Chri- ste.
-ni- te, Je- su Chri- ste.]
42
Do- mi- ne De- us, A- gnus De- i,
Do- mi- ne De- us, [A- gnus De- i,
A- gnus De- i,
Do- mi- ne De- us, [A- gnus De- i,

48

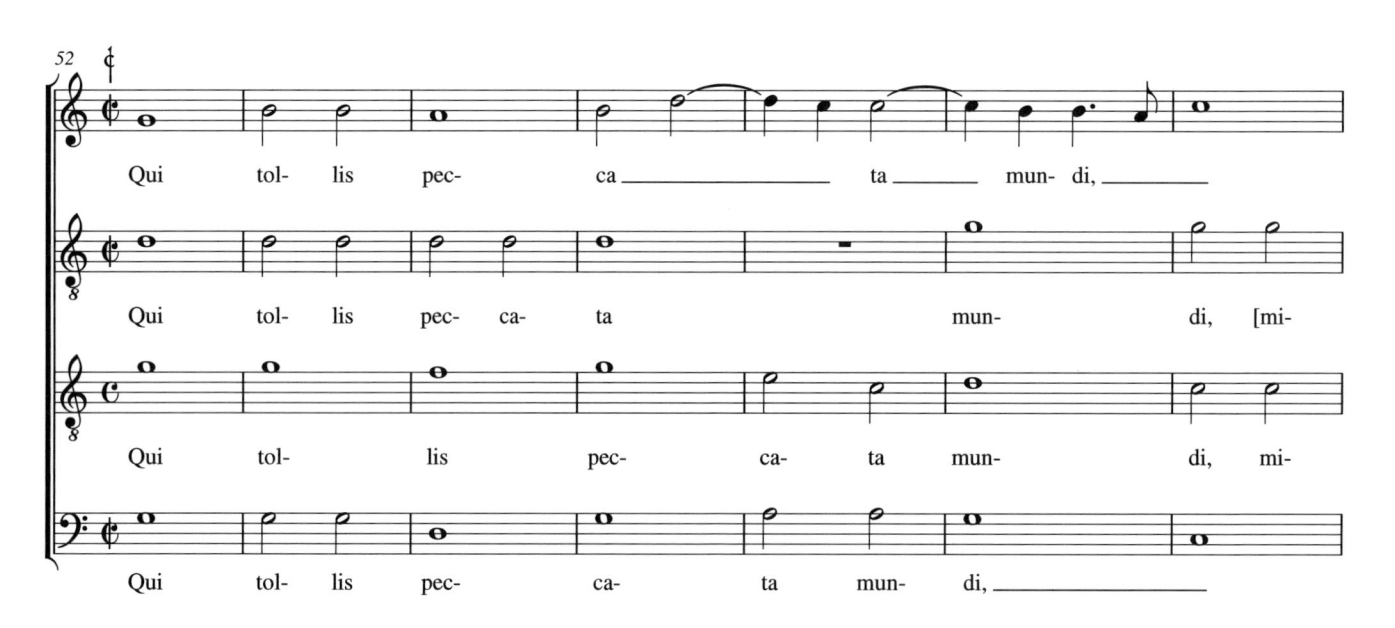

66
tol- lis pec- ca- ta mun- - di,
-lis [pec- ca- ta] su- - sci- pe de-
Qui tol- lis [pec- ca- ta su-
-lis pec- - ca- ta mun-
73
su- sci- pe de- pre- ca- ti- o-
-pre- ca- ti- o- nem no- -
-sci- pe de- pre- ca- - ti- o- nem
-di, su- - sci- pe
79
- - nem no- - - stram.
- stram, ⟨no- stram.⟩
no- - - - - - stram.]
no- - stram.]

86
Qui se- des ad dex- te- - ram Pa- tris,
Qui se- des [ad- dex- te- ram Pa- - tris,
Qui se- des [ad dex- - te- ram Pa- - tris,
94
mi- se- re- re no- - - bis. Quo-
mi- se- re- - re no- - bis. Quo-
tu
mi- se- re- re no- bis. tu
100
-ni- am tu so- lus san- ctus, tu so- lus Do- mi-
-ni- - am] tu so- lus [san- - ctus, tu so- lus] al- tis-
so- lus [san- ctus, tu so- -
so- lus san- - ctus, tu so- lus

51

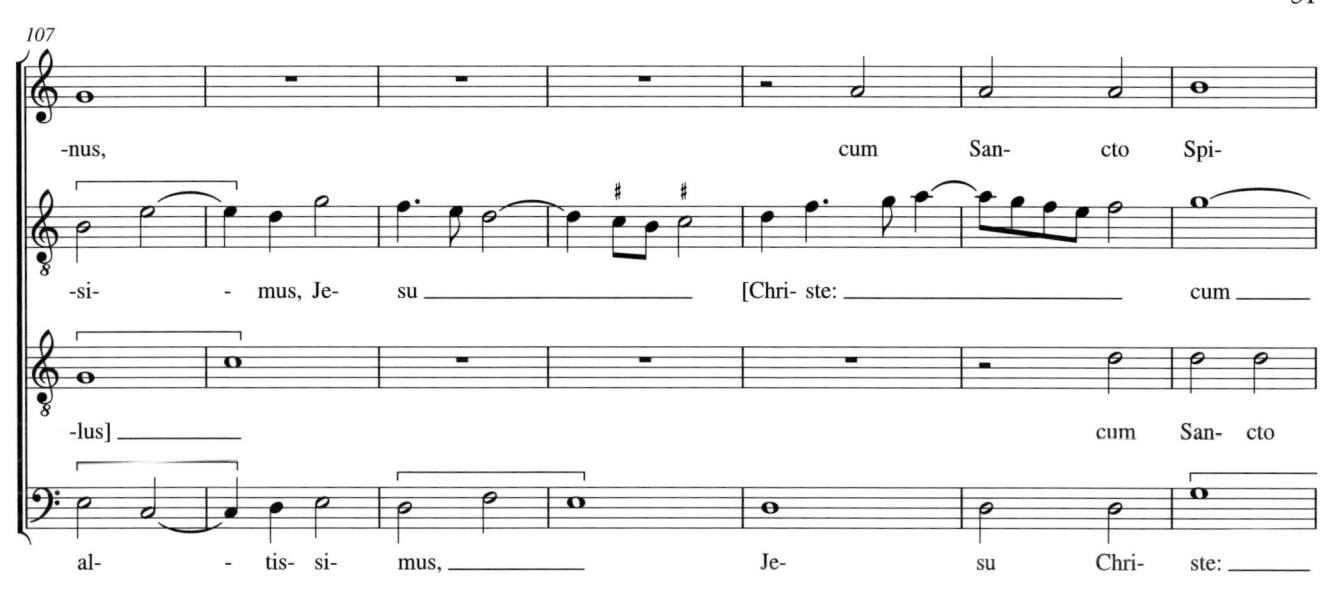

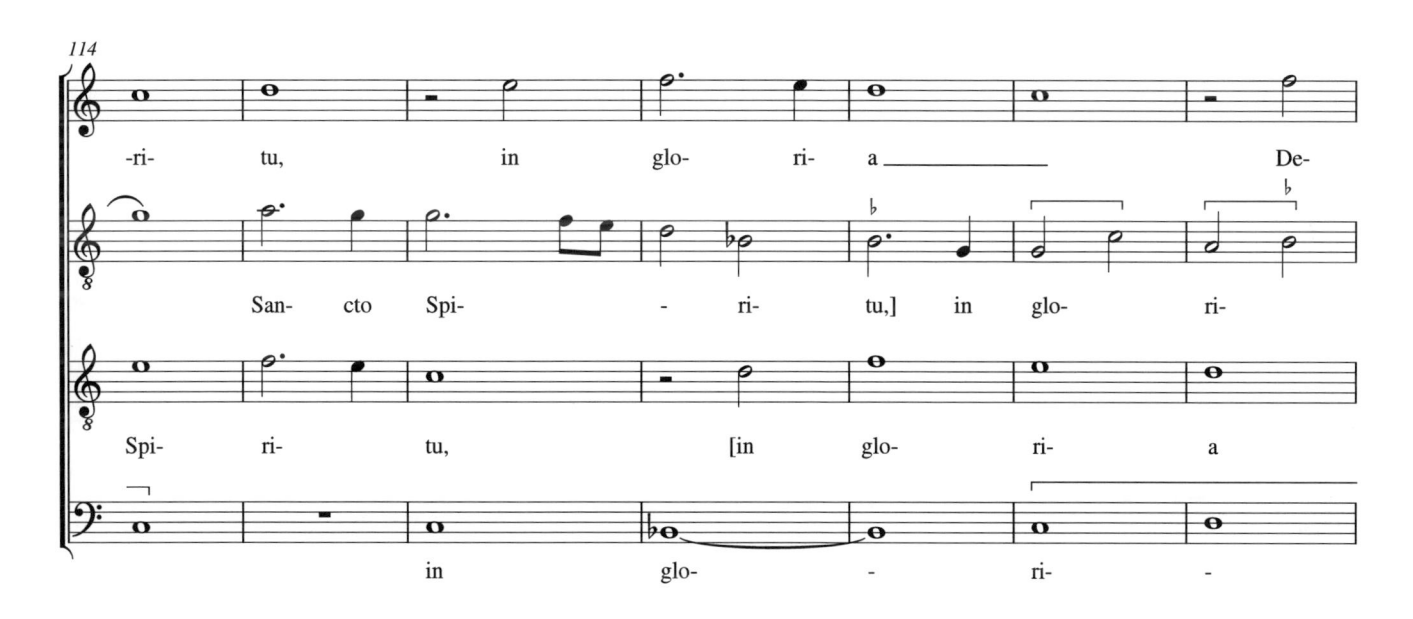

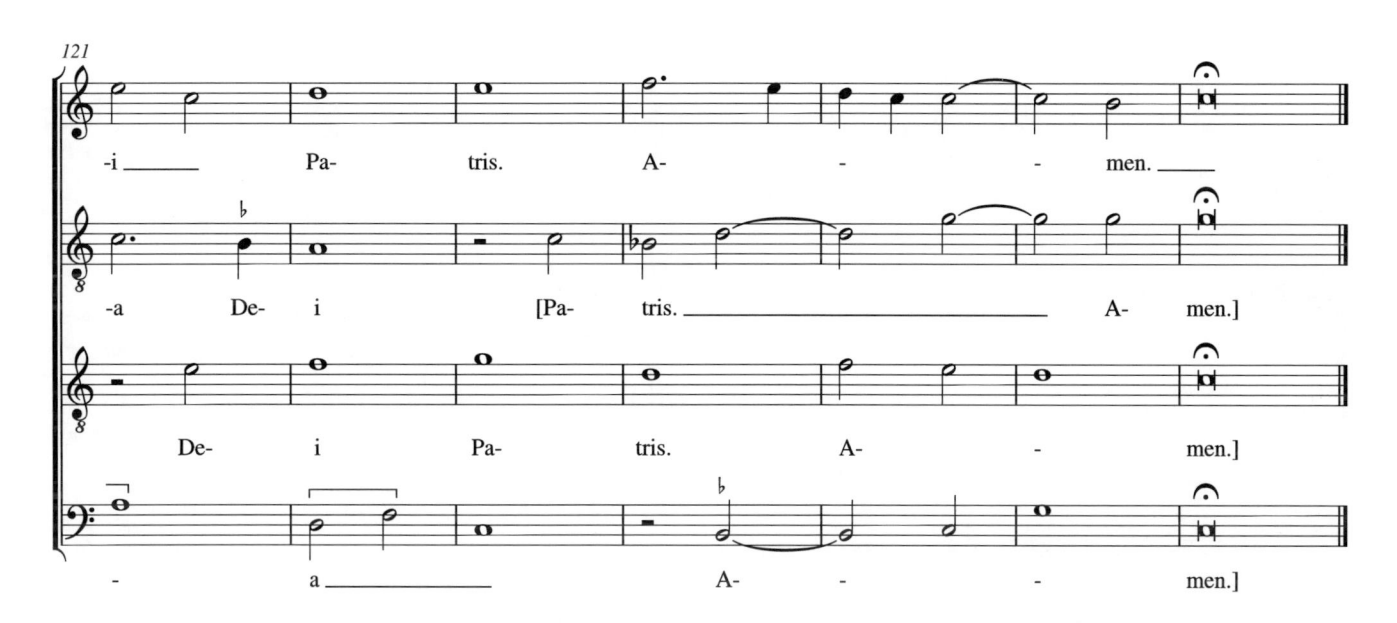

Credo

Cre-do in u-num De-um

-bi- li- um. Et in u- num Do- mi- num Je-
-um, Et in u- num Do- mi-
-bi- li- um. Et in u-
-um, Et in u- num Do- mi- num Je- sum

-sum Chri- stum, Fi- li- um De- i u- ni- ge- ni- tum,
-num Je- sum]
-num Do- mi- num Je- sum Chri- stum,
Chri- stum.]

et ex Pa- tre na- tum an- te o- mni-
et ex Pa- tre na- tum [an- te o- mni-

36
- a sae- cu- - la.
Et in- car-
- a sae- cu- - la.] Et in car-
Et in car-
41
Et in- car- na- tus est de Spi- ri- tu San-
-na- tus est [de Spi- ri- tu San-
-na- tus est [de Spi- ri- tu San- -
-na- tus est [de Spi- ri-
46
- - cto ex Ma- ri-
- - cto] ex Ma- - ri- a
- - cto] ex Ma- - ri- a Vir- gi-
-tu San- - cto] ex Ma- ri- a Vir- gi-

52
-a Vir- gi- ne, et ho- mo
Vir- gi- ne, et ho- mo fa- ctus
ne, et ho- mo [fa-
-ne, [et ho- mo fa-
57
fa- ctus est. Et re sur- re- xit
est.
-ctus est.]
-ctus est.] Et re- sur- re- xit
63
se- cun- dum Scri- ptu- ras,
ter- ti- a di- e, et a- scen- dit in cae-
ter- ti- a di- e, se- cun- dum Scri- ptu-

69
se- det ad dex- - te- ram Pa- tris.
- lum: se- det ad dex- te- ram Pa- tris. Et i-
-ras, se- det ad dex- te- ram Pa- tris. Et i-
75
ven- tu- rus est ju- di- - ca-
-te- rum cum glo- ri- - a, vi- vos
-te- rum ven- tu- rus est cum glo- ri- a, ju- -
81
-re cu- jus re- gni non e- rit fi- nis.
et mor- tu- os: cu- jus re- gni non e- rit
-di- ca- re vi- vos et mor- tu- os: cu- jus re- gni non e-

88
Et in Spi- ri- tum San-
fi- nis. [Et in Spi- ri- tum San- -
Et [in Spi- ri-
-rit [fi- nis. Et in Spi- ri- tum San- -
95
- ctum, Do- mi num, et vi- vi-
- ctum, Do- mi- - num,
-tum San- ctum, Do- - mi- num, et vi-
- ctum, Do- mi- num, et vi-
100
- fi- - can- tem, qui ex Pa- tre Fi-
et vi- vi- - fi- - can- tem, qui ex
- vi- fi- - can- tem, qui ex Pa- tre
-vi- fi- - can-tem, qui ex Pa- tre

58

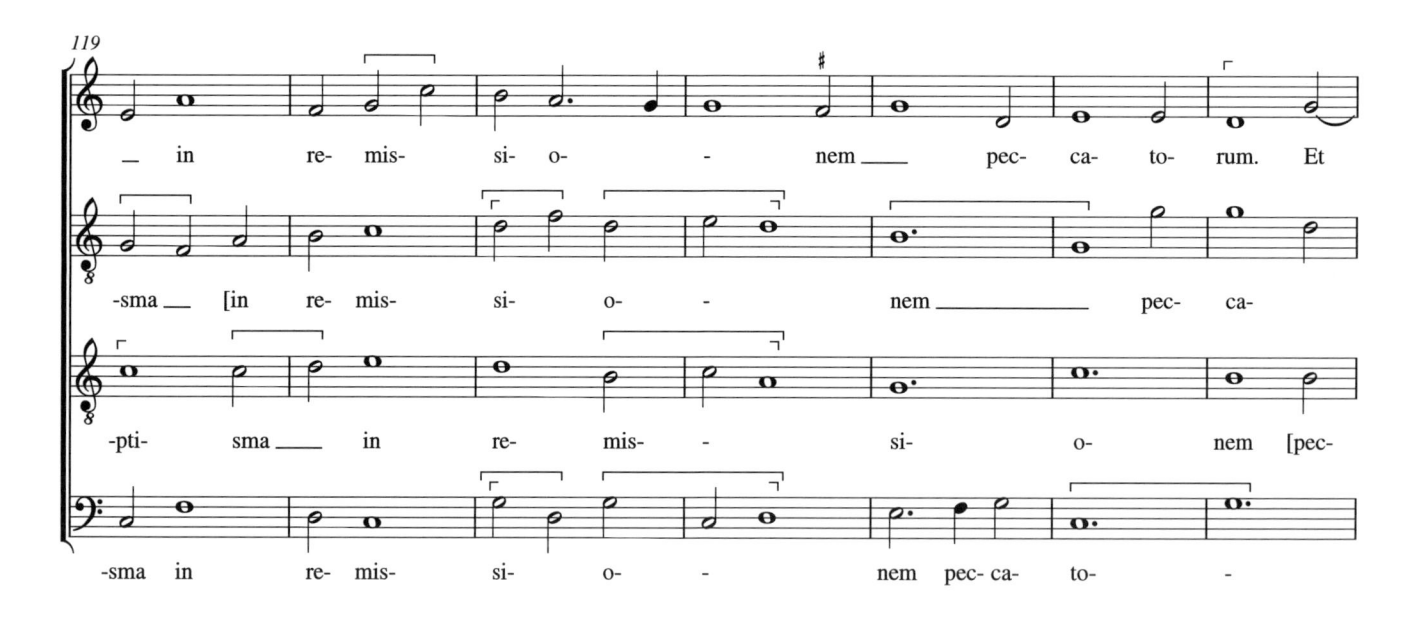

126
ex- spe- cto re- sur- re- cti- o- nem mor- tu-
-to- rum. Et ex- spe- - cto re- sur- re- cti-
-ca- to- - rum.] ___
-rum. Et ___ ex- - spe- cto re- sur- re- cti-
133
- o- rum, ___ et vi- tam ___ ven-
-o- - nem,] et vi- tam ven- tu- ri [sae- cu-
mor- tu- o- rum, ___
-o- - nem,] et vi- tam ___ ven- tu- ri ___
140
-tu- ri ___ sae- cu- li, ___ ⟨et ___ vi- tam ___
- li,] ___ ⟨et ___ vi- tam ven-
et vi- tam ven- tu- ri ___ sae- cu- li, ⟨et ___ vi-
[sae- cu- li,] ⟨et ___ vi- - - tam ven- tu-

146
ven- tu- ri- sae- cu- - li.〉
-tu- - ri〉 [sae- -
- tam ven- tu- ri sae-
-ri〉 [sae-
152
A- - - - - - men.
-cu- li. A- - - men.]
-cu- - li.〉 [A- - - - men.]
-cu- li. A- - - men.]

Sanctus

18
- - nus De- - us, ⟨Do- - mi-
De- us, Do- mi- nus
- - nus De- - -
- - nus De- -
24
- nus De- - us⟩ Sa- ba- - oth.
De- - us Sa- ba- oth.]
Pleni tacet
- us, ⟨De- us⟩ [Sa- ba- - oth.]
-us Sa- - ba- - - oth.]
31
c
[S]
CT
B
Ple- ni sunt
Ple- - ni sunt cae- -

37
cae- - li
-li
42
et ter- - - - ra
et ter- - -
48
-ra glo- ri- - - a
glo- ri- - - a
54
tu- - - - a.
[tu- - - - a.]
[tu- - - - a.]

c

60
[S]
[CT]
T
B
O- san- - na,
O- - san- na, ⟨O- san-
O- san- - na, ⟨O- san- - -
O- san- na, ⟨O- - san-
65
⟨O- san- - na
-na, O- san- - - -
- na, O- san- - -
-na, O- san- - -
70
in, in ex- cel-
- - - na⟩ in ex-
-na⟩ [in ex- cel-
- na⟩ [in ex-

74
-sis,〉 in ex- - cel- - sis.
- cel- - - sis, 〈ex- cel- sis.〉
[Benedictus tacet]
- sis, in ex- - cel- - sis.]
-cel- - - - sis.]
79
[S]
CT
B
Be- - ne di- - - - ctus,
Be- - ne- di- - -
86
〈be- - ne- - di- - ctus〉
- ctus, 〈be- ne- di- - ctus〉
92
qui ve- - - nit, 〈qui ve-
qui ve- - nit, 〈qui ve- - -

100
- - nit⟩ in no- mi-
- nit⟩ in no-
107
- - - - ne
-mi- - ne
113
3
Do- - - - mi- ni.
Osanna ut supra
[Do- - - mi- - ni.]
Osanna ut supra
Do- mi- ni, ⟨Do- mi- - - ni.⟩
[Osanna ut supra]

Agnus Dei

19
-ca- - ta mun-
-ca- - ta [mun- -
-lis pec- - ca- ta mun-
pec- ca- ta mun-
24
- di, mi- se- re- re no- - bis.
- di, mi- se- re- re no- - bis.]
Tenor tacet
- di, mi- se- re- re no- - bis.]
-di, mi- se- - re- re no- bis.]
32
c
[S]
A- gnus De- i,
CT
A- - - gnus De- i,
B
A- gnus De- - i, [qui

38
qui tol- lis pec-
qui tol- - lis
tol- lis] ⟨pec- -
44
- ca- - - ta
pec- ca- - ta
-ca- - - ta,⟩
49
⟨mun- di,⟩ mun- - - di,
mun- di, ⟨qui
pec- ca- - - ta [mun- - -
55
tol- lis pec- ca- ta mun- - di,⟩
-di, qui tol- lis] ⟨pec- ca- ta⟩ [mun-

61
⟨bis.⟩
[mi- se- - re- - re no- - bis.]
- di, mi- se- - re- - re no- - bis.]
67
c
[S]
CT
T
B
A- gnus De- i, qui
A- gnus De- - i, [qui
A- - gnus De- i, [qui
73
tol- - - - lis pec- ca-
tol- - - lis pec- ca- ta
tol- - - - lis pec- ca- ta

79
-ta mun- - - - -
mun- - - - -
mun- - - di,] do-
84
-di, do- na
-di,] ⟨do- na⟩ [no- - - bis,]
do- na ⟨no- bis, do- na⟩ no- -
- na [no- - -
89
no- - - -
⟨do- na⟩ [no- - -
-bis, ⟨do- - - -
-bis,] ⟨do- - na⟩

94
-bis, ⟨do- na no- bis pa- - cem,⟩ pa-
- bis,] ⟨do- na⟩ [no- bis
-na no- bis⟩ [pa- - - cem,
[no- - bis,] ⟨do- na⟩ [no- bis
99
- - - cem.
pa- - cem, pa- cem.]
pa- - - cem.]
pa- - - cem.]

Missa In feuers hitz
Kyrie

VerBC 759, fols. 15ᵛ–20

20
ste e- ley- son.
ste e- ley- son.
ley- son.
26
Ky- ri-
Ky- ri-
Ky- ri-
32
-e e- ley- son.
-e e- ley- son.
-e e- ley- son.

Gloria

21
pro- pter ma- gnam glo- ri- am tu- am. Do- mi- ne De- us, Rex cae-
-pter ma- gnam glo- ri- am tu- am. Do- mi- ne De- us,
-gnam glo- - ri- am tu- am. Do- mi- ne De- us,
26
- le- stis, De- us Pa- ter o- mni- po- tens. Do- mi- ne Fi-
Rex cae- le- stis, De- us Pa- ter o- mni- po- tens. Do- mi-
Rex cae- le- stis, De- us Pa- ter o- mni- - po-
31
-li u- ni- ge- ni- te, Je- su Chri- - ste.
-ne Fi- li u ni- ge- ni- te, Je- su Chri- ste.
-tens. u- ni- ge- ni- te, Je- - su Chri- ste.
36
De- i, Fi- li- us Pa- tris, mi-
De- i, Fi- li- us Pa- tris, mi- se- re- re no-
Do- mi- ne De- us, A- gnus De- i, Fi- li- - us Pa-

41
-se- re- re no- bis. Qui tol- lis pec- ca- ta [mun- di,] su- sci-
-bis. [Qui tol- lis pec- ca- ta] mun- di, su- sci- pe
- tris, Qui tol- lis pec- ca- ta mun- di, mi- se-
46
-pe Qui se- des ad dex- te- ram Pa- tris,
de- pre- ca- ti- o- nem no- stram.
-re- - re no- bis. Quo- ni- am tu
51
mi- se- re- re no- bis.
Quo- ni- am tu so- lus
mi- se- re- - re no- bis. Quo- - ni- am tu so- lus san-
so- lus san- ctus, tu so- - lus Do- mi- nus,
56
san- ctus, tu so- lus Do- mi- nus, tu so- lus al- tis- si-
-ctus, tu so- lus Do- - mi- nus, Je- su
tu so- lus al- tis- - si- mus: Je-

61
-mus: cum Sancto Spi- ri- tu, in glo- - ri-
Chri- ste, cum San- cto Spi- ri- tu, in glo- ri-
-su Chri- ste, cum San- cto Spi- ri- tu, in glo- - ri-
66
-a De- i Pa- tris. A- - men.
-a A- - - men.
-a De- i Pa- - tris. A- - men.

Credo

24
lu- men de lu- mi- ne, De- um ve- rum per quem o-
o- mni-a sae- cu- la: con- sub- stan- ti- a- lem Pa- -
-tum de De- o ve- ro, ge- ni- tum, non fa- ctum,
30
- mni- a fa- cta sunt. Qui propter nos ho- mi- nes, et
-tri, per quem o- - mni- a fa- cta sunt.
per quem o- mni- a fa- - cta sunt. [Qui pro- pter nos ho- mi-
36
pro- pter no- stram sa- lu- tem de- scen- dit de cae- lis.
et pro- pter no- stram sa- lu- tem de- scen- dit de
-nes,] et pro- pter no- stram sa- lu- tem de- scen- dit de cae-
42
Et in- car- na- tus est de Spi- ri- tu San- cto ex Ma- ri- a Vir- gi-
cae- lis de Spi- ri- tu San- cto ex Ma- ri- a Vir- gi- ne,
- lis. Et in- car- na- tus est, de Spi- ri- tu San- cto et

48
- ne, et ho- mo fa- - ctus est. Cru- ci- fi- xus et- i- am pro no-
et ho- mo fa- ctus est. Cru- - ci- -
ho- mo fa- ctus est. Cru- ci- fi- xus
55
-bis: sub Pon- ti- o Pi- la- to pas- sus, et se- pul- tus est;
-fi- - xus pas- - sus, et se- pul- tus est,
et- i- am pro no- bis sub Pon- ti- o Pi- la- to et
61
ter- ti- a di- e, et a- scen- dit in cae- lum:
se- cun- dum Scri- ptu- - ras,
re- sur- re- xit se- cun- - dum Scri- ptu- - ras, se- det
68
se- det ad dex- te- ram Pa- tris. Et i- te- rum ven- tu- rus est cum glo- ri-
vi- - - vos,
ad dex- te- ram Pa- tris. cum glo- ri-

74
-a, ju- di- ca- re cu- jus re- gni
⟨vi- vos⟩ et mor- tu- os: non
-a, ju- di- ca- re vi- vos et mor- tu- os: non e- rit
80
Et in Spi- ri- tum et vi- vi- fi- can- tem, qui
e- rit fi- nis. San- ctum, Do- mi- num,
fi- nis. Et in Spi- ri- tum qui ex Pa-
86
ex Pa- tre Fi- li- o- que pro- ce- dit. si-
qui ex Pa- tre Fi- li- o- que pro- ce- dit.
-tre Fi- li- o- que pro- - ce- dit. Qui cum Pa- tre
92
-mul a- do- - ra- tur et con- glo- ri- fi- ca- tur:
et con- glo- ri- fi- ca- tur: qui
et Fi- li- o et con- glo- ri- fi- ca- tur: qui lo- cu-

qui lo-cu-tus est per pro-phe-tas.

lo-cu-tus est per pro-phe-tas.

-tus est per pro-phe-tas. Et u-nam san-ctam ca-tho-li-cam

et a-po-sto-li-cam Ec-cle-si-am. Con-fi-te-

Et u- nam san-ctam ca-tho-li-cam Con-fi-te-or u-num ba-

Con-fi-te-or u-num ba-pti-sma

-or u-num ba-pti-sma pec-ca-to-rum.

-pti-sma in re-mis-si-o-nem re-

in re-mis-si-o-nem Et ex-spe-

mor-tu-o-rum, et vi-

-sur-rec-ti-o-nem et vi-tam

-cto et vi-tam, ⟨vi-

-tam ven-tu- - ri sae- - cu-

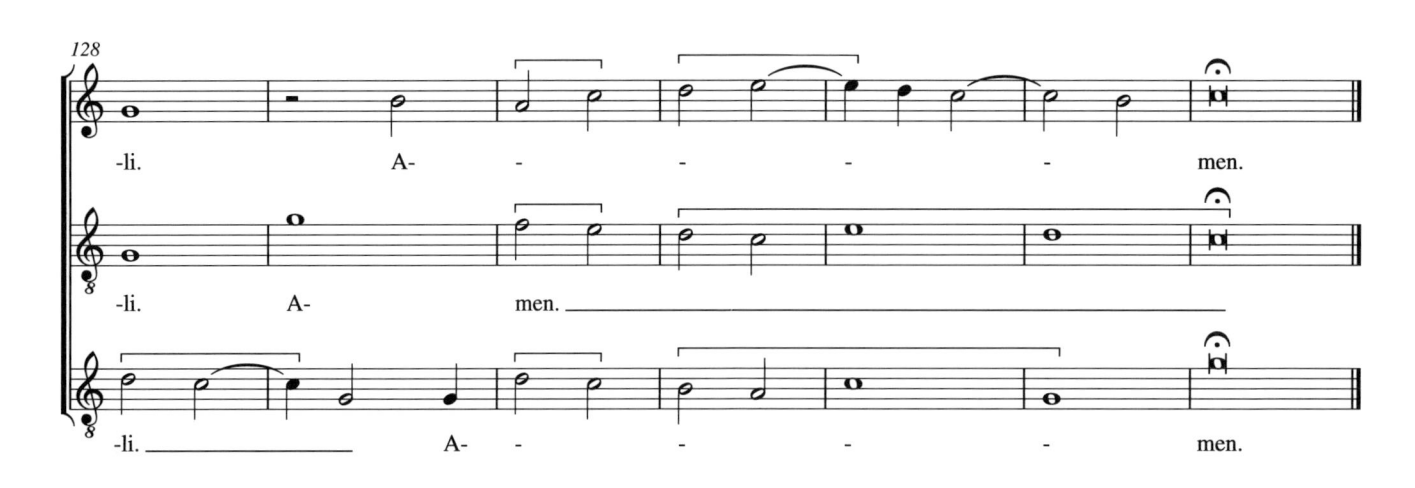

ven-tu- - ri sae- cu-

-tam) ven-tu- - ri sae-cu-

-li. A- - - - men.

-li. A- men.

-li. A- - - - men.

Sanctus

20
- ba- oth. Ple- - -
Sa- ba- oth.]
- - ba- oth.] Ple-
26
- ni sunt cae- - -
-ni sunt cae-
32
- - - - li
- - - - li
38
et ter- - - ra glo- -
et ter- ra glo- - -

44
- - ri- a tu- - - -
- ri- a tu- - - -
50
- - a. O- - san- -
O- - san- -
- - a. O- san- -
56
- - - - na in ex-
- - na
- na, ⟨O- - - sa- na⟩ in
63
-cel- - - - - - -
in ex- cel- - - - -
ex- cel- - - - - -

-sis. Be- ne- di-
-sis.
-sis. Be-
-ne- di-
-ctus qui ve-
-ctus qui
-nit in no-
ve- nit in no-

89

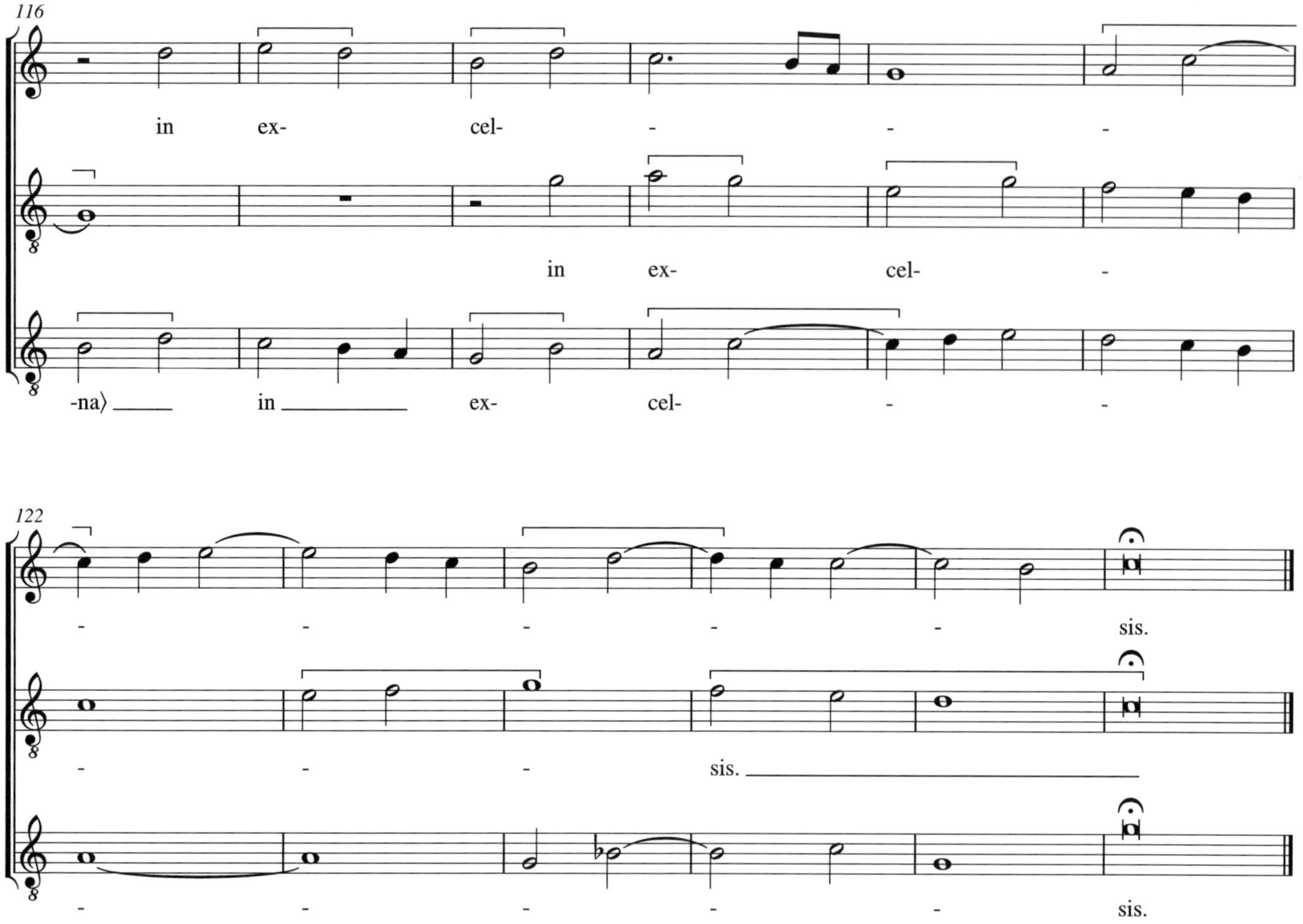
116
in ex- cel- - - -
in ex- cel- -
-na⟩ in ex- cel- - -
122
- - - - - sis.
- - - sis.
- - - - - sis.

Agnus Dei

13
re-
no-
re, mi- se- re-
bis, do- na no-

17
-re no- bis.
-bis pa- cem.]
-re no- bis.]
-bis pa- cem.]
-re no- bis, no- bis.]
-bis pa- cem, pa- cem.]

Missa La Martinella
Kyrie

VatS 35, fols. 38ᵛ–52

18
Ky- - ri- e e-
- - son, Ky- - ri- e
- son, ⟨Ky- - ri- e
- ri- - e, Ky- - ri- e e-
23
-ley- - - - son.⟩
e- ley- - - - son.⟩
Christe tacet
e- ley- - - son.⟩
- ley- - - - - son.⟩
29
S
Chri- ste, ⟨Chri- - - ste⟩ e- ley- -
CT
Chri- ste, ⟨Chri- - - - ste⟩ e- ley-
B

36
-son,
-son, Chri- - - - ste, Chri- - - ste,
Chri- - - - ste, Chri- - -
43
⟨Chri- - - ste e- - - ley-
Chri- - - ste e- ley- - -
-ste, Chri- - - ste e- ley- -
49
-son, Chri- - - ste,
-son, Chri- - - ste, Chri- - -
-son, Chri- - - ste, Chri- - -
55
Chri- ste e- ley- - - son,
- - ste e- - ley- - son, Chri-
- - ste e- ley- - - son, Chri-

62
Chri- - - ste e-
- - ste, Chri- - - ste
- - ste, Chri- - ste e-
68
- ley- - - son, e- - ley- son.⟩
e- ley- - - son, e- ley- - son.⟩
- ley- - - son, e- ley- son.⟩
74
S
Ky- ri- - e e-
CT
Ky- ri- e e- ley- - son, ⟨e- ley-
T
Ky-
B
Ky- ri- e e- ley- - son, ⟨e- ley- son,

79
-ley- - son, ⟨e- - ley-
- - son, e- ley-
- ri- e e- ley-
e- ley- son, e- ley-
83
- son, Ky- - ri- e
- son, Ky- - ri- e e- ley-
- son,
- son, Ky- - ri- e e- - ley- son,
87
e- ley- son, Ky- ri- e e- ley- son.⟩
- son, Ky- ri- e e- ley- son.⟩
⟨Ky- ri- e e- ley- son, Ky- ri- - e e- ley- son.⟩
Ky- ri- e e- ley- son.⟩

Gloria

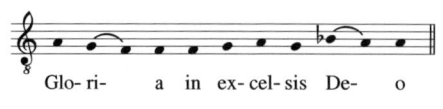

18
- tis. be- ne- di- ci- mus te,
Lau- da- - - mus te, be- ne- di-
be- - ne-
-tis. Lau- da- - - mus te, be- ne- di- ci-
24
a- do- ra- mus te,
- ci- mus te, a- do- ra-
- di- - ci- - mus
- mus te, a- do- ra- - mus te,
29
glo- ri- fi- - ca- - - mus te. Gra-
- mus te, glo- - ri- fi- ca- - mus te. Gra- - ti-
te, [glo- ri- fi- ca- mus te. Gra-
glo- ri- fi- - ca- mus te. Gra- -

34
-ti- as a- - gi- mus ti- - - bi
- as a- gi- mus ti- -
-ti- as a- gi- - mus
- ti- as, a- - gi- mus ti- - -
40
pro- pter ma- - gnam glo- ri- am tu- am.
-bi pro- - pter ma- - gnam glo- - ri- am tu-
ti- bi pro- - pter ma- gnam
-bi [pro- - pter ma- - gnam glo- - ri- am tu-
45
Do- mi- ne De- - us,
- am. [Do- - mi- ne De- us, Rex cae- le- -
- am, Do- mi- ne De- us, Rex cae- le- -

50
Pa- ter o- - mni- po- tens. Do- - mi- ne
-stis,] De- us Pa- ter o- mni- po- tens. Do- - mi- ne
-stis, De- us Pa- ter o- - mni- po- tens. Do- mi- ne
56
Fi- li u- ni- ge- - ni- te,
Fi- li u- ni- - ge- ni- te, Je-
Fi- - li u- ni- ge- ni- te,
Fi- li u- ni- ge- ni- te, Je- -
61
Je- su Chri- ste. Do- - - mi-
- su Chri- - ste. Do- - -
Je- su Chri- ste. Do- - mi- -
- su Chri- ste. Do- - - mi-

67
-ne De- - - - us,
- mi- ne De- - - us, A-
-ne, A-
-ne De- - - - us,
72
A- gnus De- - - i, Fi-
- gnus De- - - i, Fi-
- gnus De- - i,
A- gnus De- - i, Fi- - li-
77
- li- us Pa- - tris.
-li- us Pa- - tris, ⟨Pa- - tris.⟩
Fi- li- - us Pa- - tris.]
-us Pa- - - tris.]

82
Qui tol- - lis pec-
Qui tol- - lis pec- ca- - - - -
Qui tol- - lis pec- ca-
89
-ca- ta mun- - di, mi- se- re- re no-
-ta mun- - di, [mi- - se- re-
pec- - ca-
- ta mun- di,
95
- bis. Qui tol- lis pec- ca- ta mun- di
-re no- bis. Qui tol- lis pec- ca- ta mun- di,
- ta mun- - di
[Qui tol- - lis pec- ca- ta mun- di,

102
su- - sci- pe de- pre- ca- ti- - o- nem no-
su- - sci- pe de- - pre- - ca- ti- o-
[su- - sci- pe de- pre- ca- ti-
su- - sci- pe de- - pre- ca- ti- o-
110
- - - - - -
-nem no- - - - -
-o- - nem no- - -
-nem no- - - -
116
-stram.
-stram.] Qui se- - -
-stram.
-stram. Qui se- -

123
ad dex- - te- ram Pa-
-des [ad dex- te- ram Pa- -
- - - des ad dex- te- - ram,]
129
- - - tris, mi- - se- re- re no- bis. Quo-
- - - tris, mi- se- re- re] Quo-
mi- - se- re-
mi- se- re- re no- bis. [Quo-
136
- ni- am tu so- lus san- - - -
- ni- am tu so- lus san- ctus, tu
- re no- bis.
- ni- am tu so- lus san- ctus, tu so- lus

143
- ctus, tu so-
so- - lus san- ctus,
san- - - ctus, tu so-
149
- lus
[tu so- -
tu so-
- lus, tu so- - - -
154
Do- - - - mi- nus,
- lus Do- - mi-
- - - - lus
- lus Do- - mi- nus, Do- -

159
⟨tu so- - lus
- nus, tu so- - lus Do- -
Do- mi-
- mi- nus, tu so- - lus Do- -
164
Do- - - mi- nus, Do- - - mi-
- mi- - - nus, Do- - mi-
- nus,]
- mi- - nus,]
170
-nus,⟩ tu so- lus
-nus,] tu so- - - - -
tu so- lus, ⟨tu so- -

176
al- ti- - -
- - lus al- ti- -
- - lus⟩ al- tis-
182
-si- mus, Je- - su Chri- - ste.
- si- mus, Je- - su Chri- - ste.
Je- - su Chri- - ste.
- si- mus, Je- - su Chri- - ste.
190
c
Cum San- - - cto Spi-
Cum San- - - - -
Cum San- - - cto Spi-

-cto, ⟨cum San- -ri-tu, in glo- -ri-a De- -

cum San- -cto Spi- -ri-tu, in glo- -ri-a De- -

Cum San- -cto Spi- -ri-tu, [in glo- -ri-a

-ri- -tu: [in glo- -ri- -a De-

110

-i Pa - - - tris. A-
-i Pa - - - tris.
De - i Pa - - tris.
-i Pa - - - tris.] A-

- - - - - men.
A - - - men.
A - - - men.]
- - - - - men.

Credo

Cre-do in u-num De-um

17
-bi- li- um. Et in u- num Do- - mi- num Je- sum
-bi- li- um. Et in u- num Do- mi- num Je- sum
-bi- li- um. Et in u- num Do- mi- num Je- sum
22
Chri- stum, Fi- li- um De- - i u- ni-
Chri- stum, Fi- - li- um De- - i u-
u- -
Chri- stum, Fi- li- - um De- - i u-
27
- ge- - - ni- tum,
-ni- ge- - ni- tum, [an- te
-ni- ge- - ni- tum, [et ex
-ni- ge- ni- tum, et ex Pa- tre na- tum an-

32
an- te o- mni- a sae- - cu-
o- mni- a sae- cu- la.
Pa- tre
- te o- mni- a sae- - cu-
36
-la: De- - um de De- o, lu-
De- um de De- - o, lu-
De-
-la: De- - um de De- o,
40
-men de lu- - mi- ne, ge- ni- tum,
- men de lu- - mi- ne,]
-um de De- o, lu- men de lu- - mi-
lu- men de- lu- - - mi-

45
non fa- ctum, con- sub-stan- ti- a- lem Pa-
con- sub-stan- ti- a- - lem Pa- tri, [o- - mni-
-ne,
-ne, con- sub- stan- ti- a- lem Pa- - -
50
-tri, per quem o- mni- a fa- cta sunt. Qui pro-
-a fa- - cta sunt.] Qui pro-
fa- - - cta sunt. Qui pro-
- - - - tri, Qui pro-
56
- pter nos ho- - -
- pter nos ho- - - -
- pter nos
- pter nos ho- - -

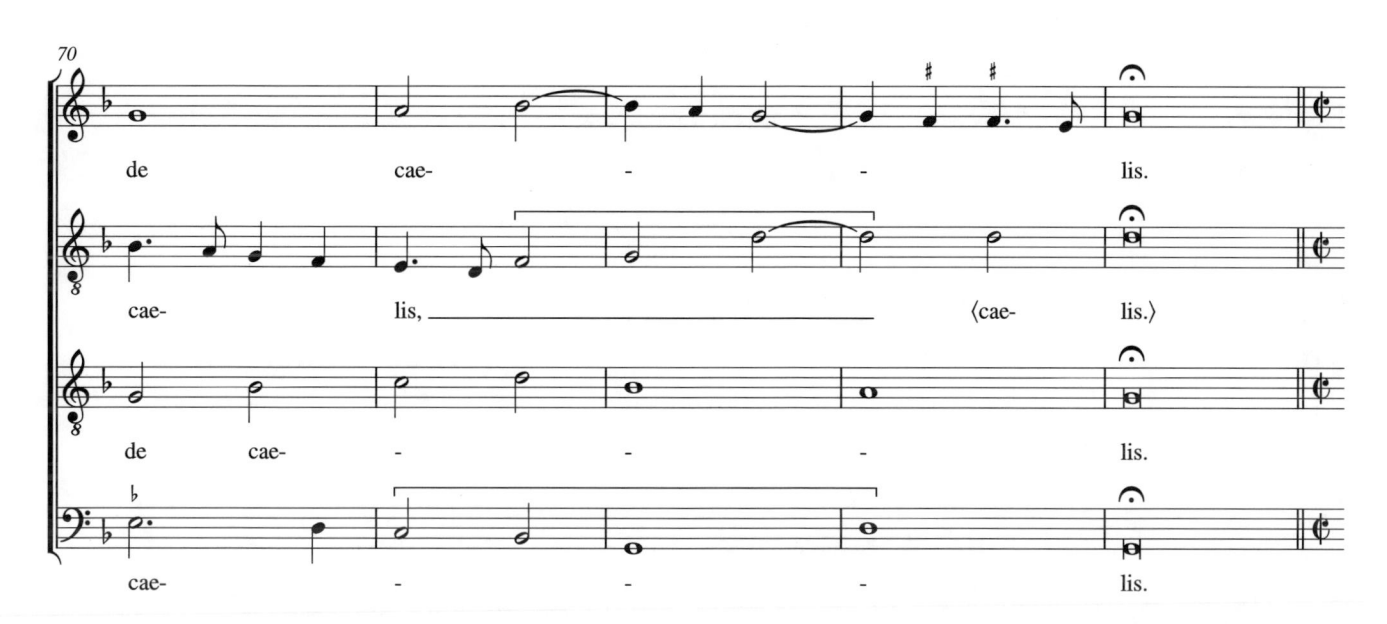

-mines, et propter nostram salu-
-mines, et pro- -pter nostram sa-
et pro- pter nostram sa- lu-
-mi- nes,] et pro- pter no- stram

-tem de- scen- - - dit
-lu- tem de- scen- - dit de
-tem] de- scen- dit
sa- lu- tem de- scen dit de

de cae- - - lis.
cae- lis, ⟨cae- lis.⟩
de cae- - - - lis.
cae- - - - - lis.

75
Et in- car- na- tus est, ⟨et in- - car- na-
Et in- car- na- tus
81
- - tus est, et in- car-
est, ⟨in- car- - na- tus, et in- car- na- -
Et in- car- na- - -
86
-na- - - tus est⟩
- tus est, et in- car- na- - tus est⟩
Et in- car- - na- - tus
-tus est, ⟨et in- car- na- - - tus

91
de
[de Spi- ri- - tu, de Spi- -
est
[de Spi- -
est⟩ [de Spi- ri- tu,
de
96
Spi- - -
- ri- tu
Spi- -
- ri- tu,
Spi- -
Spi-
101
- ri- - - tu
- - - - -
- ri- - tu,
Spi- ri-
- ri- tu,
Spi- ri-

106
[San- - cto, San- -
- tu San- - - -
- tu San- - cto,
- tu San- - cto, San-
111
- - cto,] ⟨Spi-
- cto, Spi- - - ri- tu
- - cto, Spi- - ri- tu
117
- ri- - tu⟩ [San-
San- cto, Spi- - - ri-
San- cto, Spi- ri- -

[Sheet music, measures 122–136]

Text underlay:
- ...cto] ex
- -tu San- - - -cto ex
- San- - - - - - - -
- -tu San- - - - - - -

- Ma- ri- - a Vir- - -
- Ma- ri- - a Vir- gi- - - - -
- -cto Vir- -
- -cto ex Ma- ri- - a Vir- -

- -gi- ne, ⟨Ma- ri- a Vir- - -gi-
- -ne, Ma- - ri- a, Ma- ri-
- -gi- ne, Ma- ri- a Vir- gi-
- -gi- ne, Ma- ri- - - - a

138
-ne, Ma- ri- a Vir-
-a Vir- gi- ne, Ma- ri- a Vir-
ne, Ma- ri-
Vir- gi- ne, Vir-
143
gi- ne.〉
gi- ne.]
-a Vir- gi- ne.]
gi- ne.]
148
Et ho- mo fa- ctus est.
Et ho- mo fa- ctus est.
Et ho- mo fa- ctus est.
Et ho- mo fa- ctus est.

121

122

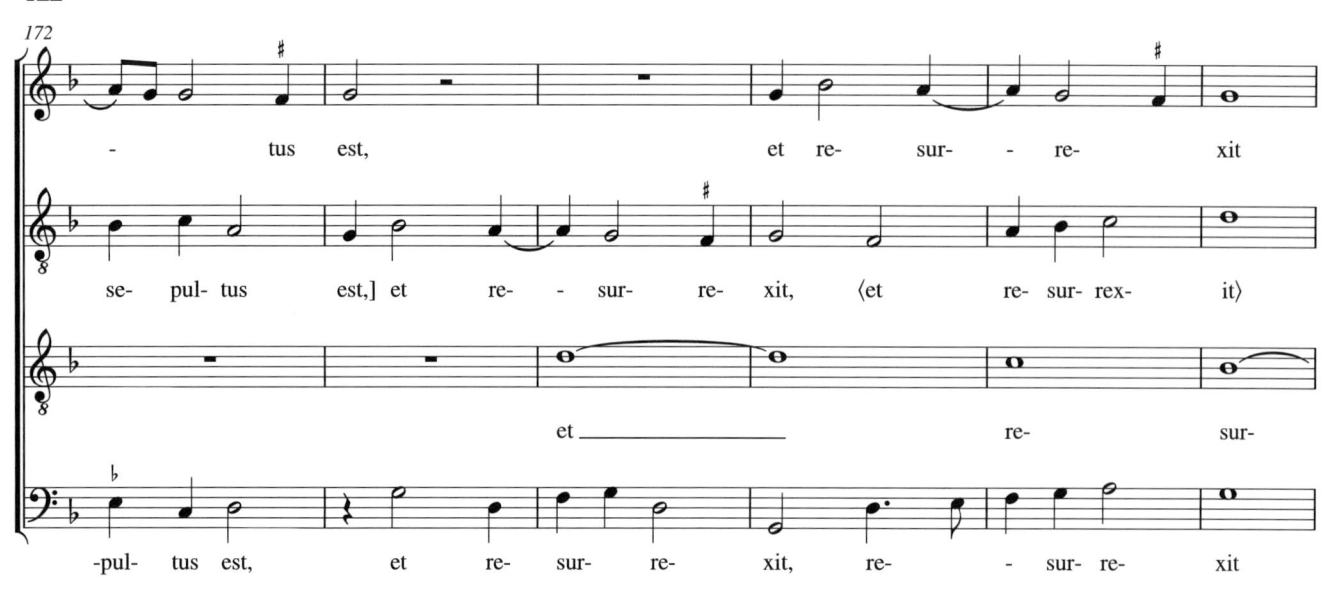

190
-lum: se- det ad dex- te- ram Pa- tris.
cae- lum: [se- - det ad dex- - te- ram Pa- tris, Pa- -
in cae- lum: Et i-
[se- det ad dex- te- -
196
Et i- te- - rum ven- tu- rus est cum
-tris.] Et i- te- - rum ven- tu- rus est cum
-te- - - rum ven- tu- rus
- ram Pa- tris.] Et
202
glo- - ri- - a, ju- - di- ca-
glo- - ri- a, ju- di- ca-
est cum glo- ri- a,
i- - te- rum [est cum

-re vi- vos et mor- tu- os:
-re vi- vos et mor- tu-
glo- ri- a,] ju- di- ca- re vi- vos et mor- tu-

cu- jus re- gni
-os: cu- jus re- gni
non
-os: cu- jus re- gni non

non e- rit fi- nis, ⟨fi- nis.⟩
non e- rit fi- nis.
e- rit fi- nis.
e- rit fi- nis. [Et in Spi-

225
[Et in Spi- - ri- tum San- ctum,]
Et in Spi- ri- tum San- ctum, Do- -
Et in Spi- ri- tum San- ctum,
- ri- tum San- ctum, et in Spi- ri- tum San- ctum, Do-
230
Do- mi- num, et vi- vi- fi- can-
- mi- num, et vi- vi- fi- can- - -
Do- mi- num, et vi- vi- fi- can- tem,
-mi- num, et vi- vi- fi- can- - -
235
-tem,
-tem, [qui ex Pa- tre Fi- li- o- - - que pro- ce-
-tem, qui ex Pa- tre Fi- li- o- que pro- ce-

240
Qui cum Pa- tre et ___ Fi- li- o ·si- mul a- do- - ra-
- - dit. si- mul a- do- ra-
- - dit. si- - mul a- do- - ra-
245
-tur, et con- glo- ri- - fi- ca- tur. Et ___ u- nam san-
-tur, Et u- nam san-
-tur, et ___ con- glo- ri- fi- ca- tur. Et u- nam San-
250
-ctam ca- tho- li- cam et a- po- sto- li- cam Ec- cle- - si-
-ctam ca- tho- li- cam et a- po- sto- li- cam Ec- cle- - si-
-ctam ca- tho- - li- cam] Ec- - cle- - si-

255
-am. Con- - fi- te- or, ⟨con- fi-
-am.] Con- fi- - te- or
Con- - fi- - - te- or,
-am. Con- - fi- - - te- or
260
- te- or⟩ u- num ba- pti- sma
u- num ba- - pti- - sma [in
u- - num ba-
[ba- pti- - sma
266
in re- mis- si- o- nem pec- ca- to-
re- mis- si- o- nem pec- ca- - -
- pti- sma in re- mis- si- - o-
in re- mis- si- o- -

271
-rum. Et ex- spe- cto re- sur- re- cti- o-
-to- rum. Et ex- spe- cto re- sur- re- cti-
-nem ex- spe- cto re- - sur-
-nem Et ex- spe- cto re- sur- re- cti- o-
276
- nem mor- tu- o- -
-o- nem mor- tu- o- -
-re- cti- o- nem
- nem mor- tu- o- -
281
-rum, et vi- tam ven- tu ri
-rum,] et vi- tam ven- tu- - ri,
-rum,] et vi- tam ven- - tu- ri,

287
sae- cu-
⟨et vi- tam ven- tu- ri⟩ sae-
et vi- tam ven- tu- ri
⟨et vi- tam ven- tu- - ri⟩ sae-
293
-li. A- -
- - cu- li. A-
sae- - cu- li. A-
- - - cu- li. A-
298
- - - men, ⟨A- men.⟩
- - - men, ⟨A- men.⟩
- - - men, A- men.]
- - men, ⟨A- men.⟩

Sanctus

17
ctus,
ctus, San-
ctus,
ctus,
22
San- ctus,⟩ Do-
ctus, San- ctus,⟩
⟨San- ctus,⟩ [Do-
San- ctus,⟩
27
mi- nus De-
Do- mi- nus De-
mi- nus
Do- mi- nus De-

132

133

66
cae- - li, ⟨cae- -
- - - li, ⟨cae- -
- - - li
72
- - - li⟩
- - - li⟩ et ter-
et ter-
77
et ter- -
- - - ra, ⟨et ter- -
- - - ra,
82
- - ra, ⟨et ter- - -
- - ra, et
⟨et ter- - - ra⟩

135

109
S
[O- san- - - na,
CT
[O- - san- - - - na, O- - san-
T
B
O- - san- -
116
O- san- - na, O- - san-
- - - na, O- - san-
O- -
- - - na, ⟨O- - san-
121
-na, O- - san- na, O- - san- -
-na, O- - san- na, O- san- - - - -
-san- - na, ⟨O- san- - - -
-na, O- san- na, O- -

129
-na, O- - - san-
- - - na, O- san- - -
- na, O- - san- - -
- - - san- - - -
136
- - - - -
- - - - -
- - - - -
- - - na, O- san-
141
- - - -
- na, O- san- -
- - na〉
- na, O- san- -

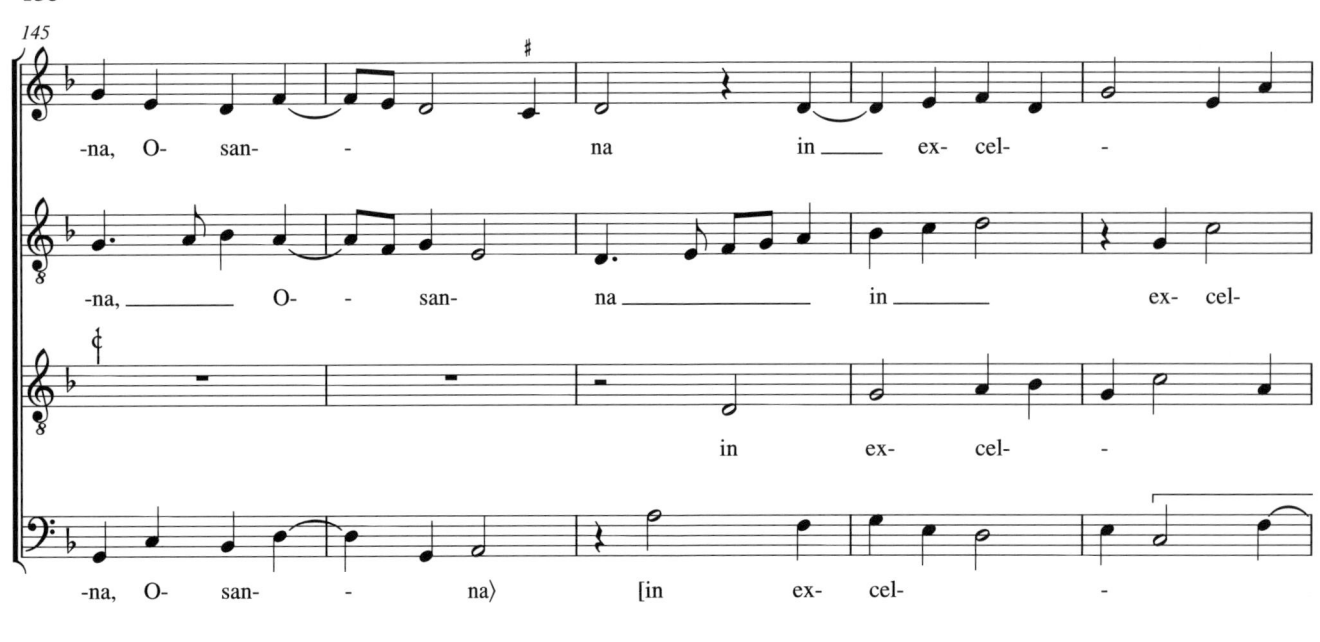

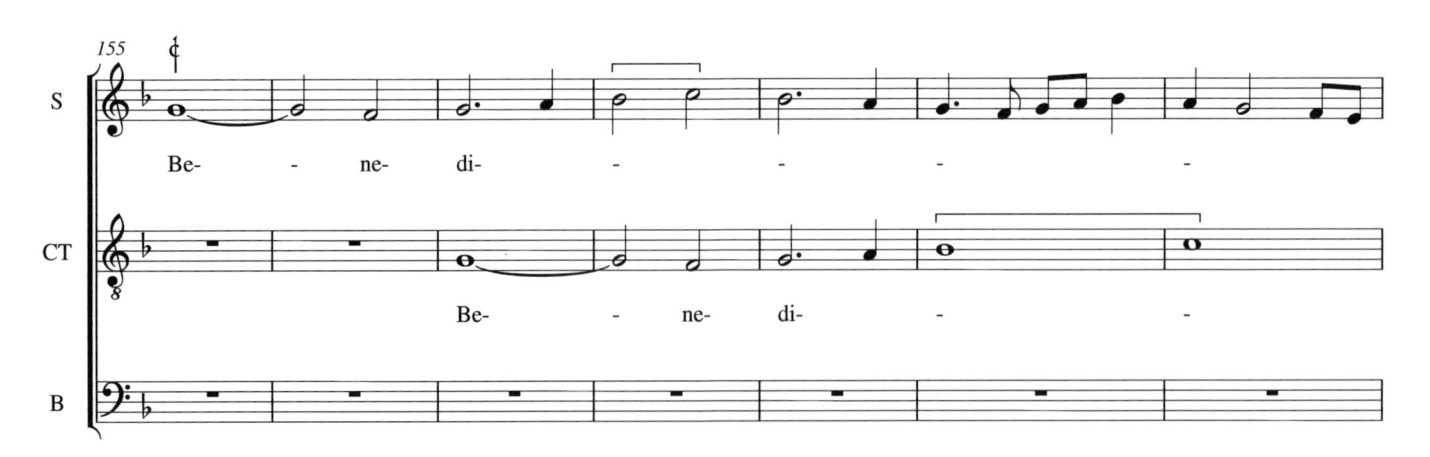

-na, O- san - na in ex- cel -
-na, O- san - na in ex- cel -
in ex- cel -
-na, O- san - na⟩ [in ex- cel -

- - - sis.]
- - sis, ex- cel - sis.]

Benedictus tacet

- - - - sis.
- - sis, in ex- cel - sis.]

S: Be- ne- di- - - - -
CT: Be- ne- di- - -
B:

162
-ctus, ⟨be- ne- di- - -
- - ctus, ⟨be-
168
- - - - - -
-ne- di- - - - -
174
- ctus⟩ [qui ve- - nit]
- ctus⟩ qui ve- nit, ⟨qui ve-
qui ve- nit,
180
- - - - -
⟨qui ve- - - -

185
in no- - -
- - nit⟩ [in no- mi- ne, in no- -
- - nit⟩
191
-mi- - - - ne,
- - - - mi- ne, no-
in no- mi- ne, ⟨in no- - mi- ne,
196
⟨in no- - mi- ne⟩
-mi- ne, no- - - mi- ne, no-
in no- - mi- ne, in no-
201
Do- - - mi- ni,
- - mi- ne] Do- - mi- ni, ⟨Do-
- mi- ne⟩ Do-

141

Agnus Dei

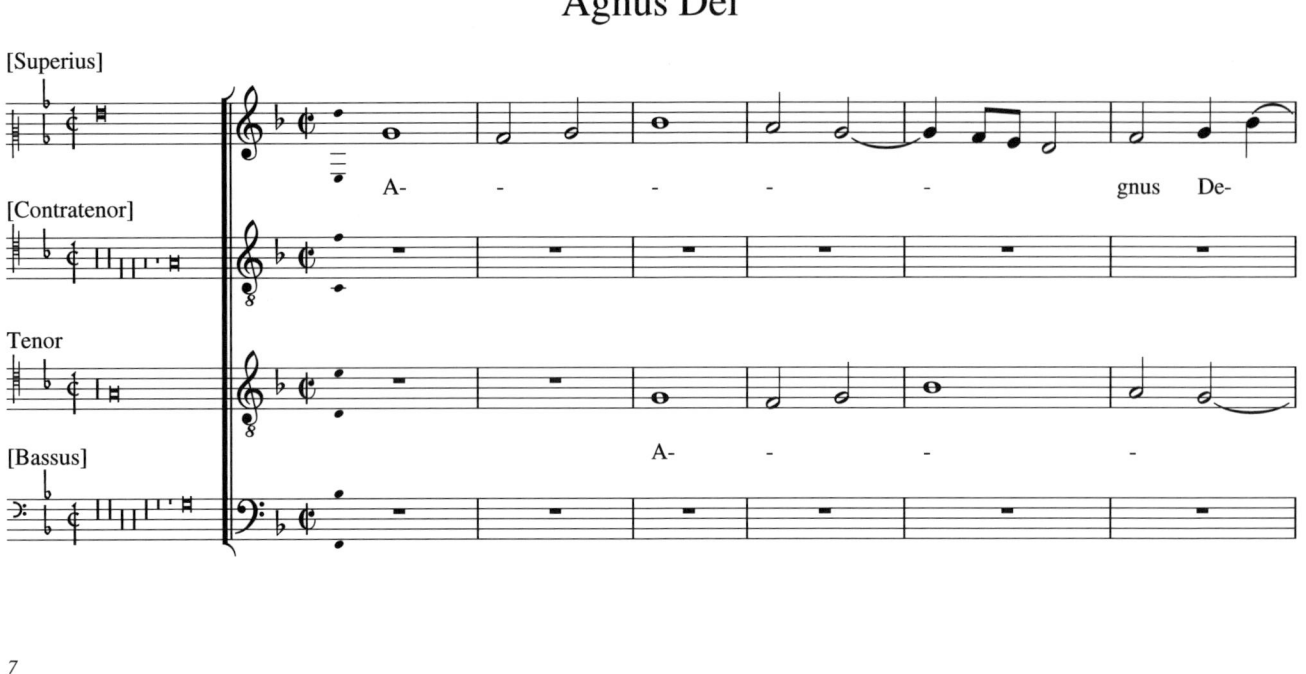

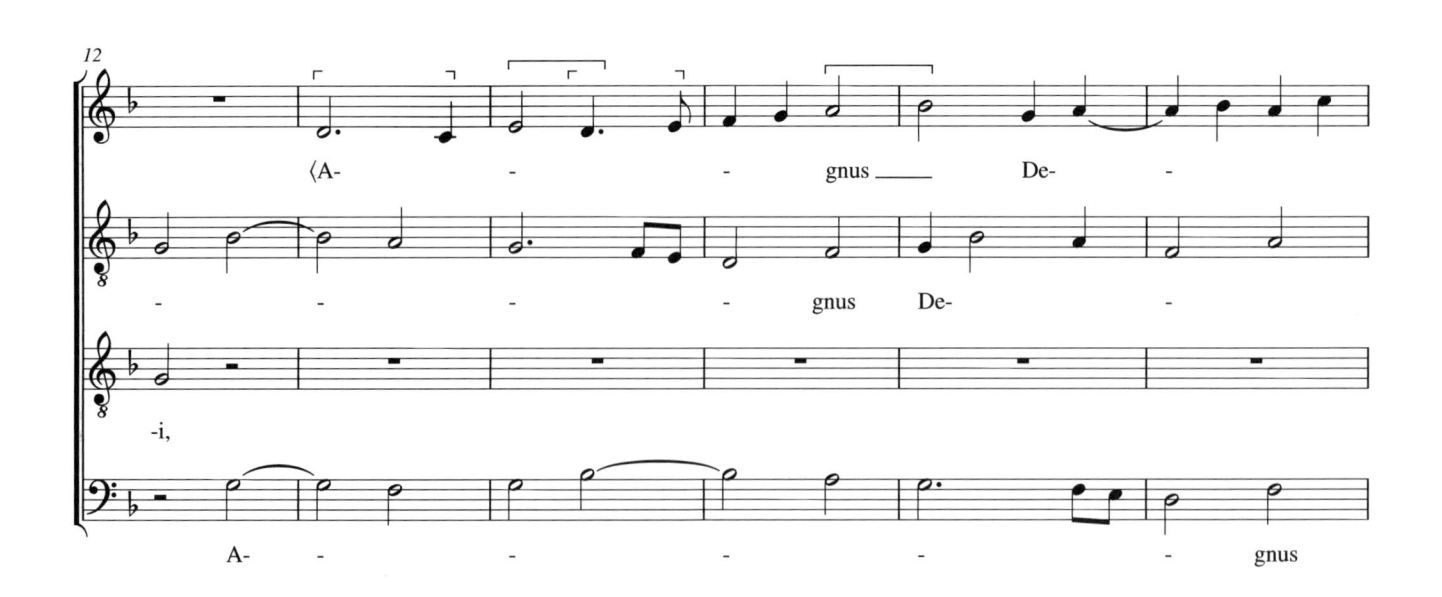

18
- - i,⟩ [qui
- - i,
qui tol- -
De- - i, qui tol-
22
tol- - - lis,
[qui tol- - - - lis, qui
- - lis, qui
- - lis, ⟨qui tol- - lis, qui
27
qui tol- - - lis
tol- - lis pec-
tol- - - - -
tol- - - lis, qui tol- -

32
pec- ca- ta, pec- ca- -
-ca- - ta, pec- ca- -
-lis
-lis⟩ [pec- ca- ta, pec- ca- - -
37
-ta
-ta, pec- ca- - ta, pec- ca- -
pec- ca- - ta
-ta, pec- ca- - ta, pec- ca-
42
pec- ca- - ta mun-
-ta mun- - di, mun- - -
mun- - - di,]
-ta mun- - di, mun- - - di,]

145

63
gnus, ⟨A-
gnus,
68
gnus, A-
⟨A- gnus, A-
73
-gnus⟩ De-
gnus, A- gnus⟩ De-
78
-i, ⟨De-
-i, De- i, De-

84
- i, A- - gnus De- - -
- i, A- - gnus De- -
89
- i,〉 qui tol-
- i,〉 [qui tol- - lis,
Qui tol- - lis, 〈qui
94
- - lis, 〈qui tol- - -
qui tol- - - lis, qui tol-
tol- - lis, qui tol- - -
99
-lis〉
-lis pec- - ca- - -
-lis〉 [pec- ca- - - - ta,

104
-ta, pec- ca- - - -
pec- ca- - - - -
109
- - ta mun- - -
- ta mun- - - di
114
-di, mun- - di, mun- - di, mun- di, mun-
pec- ca- ta, pec- - ca- ta, pec- ca- ta, pec- - ca- ta
120
[bis.]
- di,] mi- se- - re- - re no- - bis.
mun- di] mi- se- re- - re no- - bis.

126
S
CT
T
B
A- - gnus, ⟨A- -
A- - - - - -
A- - - gnus
A- - - - -
132
- - gnus⟩ De-
- gnus, ⟨A- - - - - gnus⟩
- gnus, ⟨A- - - - gnus⟩
137
- - - i, ⟨De- i,⟩
De- -
De- - - - i,
De- - - i, ⟨De-

142
qui tol- - -
- - i, qui tol- - -
qui tol- - - lis,
- - i,⟩ qui [tol- lis,] ⟨qui⟩ [tol-
147
-lis, ⟨qui tol- - lis, qui tol-
-lis, ⟨qui tol- - - - -
⟨qui tol- - lis, qui tol- -
-lis,] ⟨qui⟩ [tol- - lis,] ⟨qui⟩
152
- - lis⟩ [pec-
- - lis⟩ pec- ca- ta mun-
- lis⟩ pec- ca-
[tol- - lis] pec- ca- - ta

151

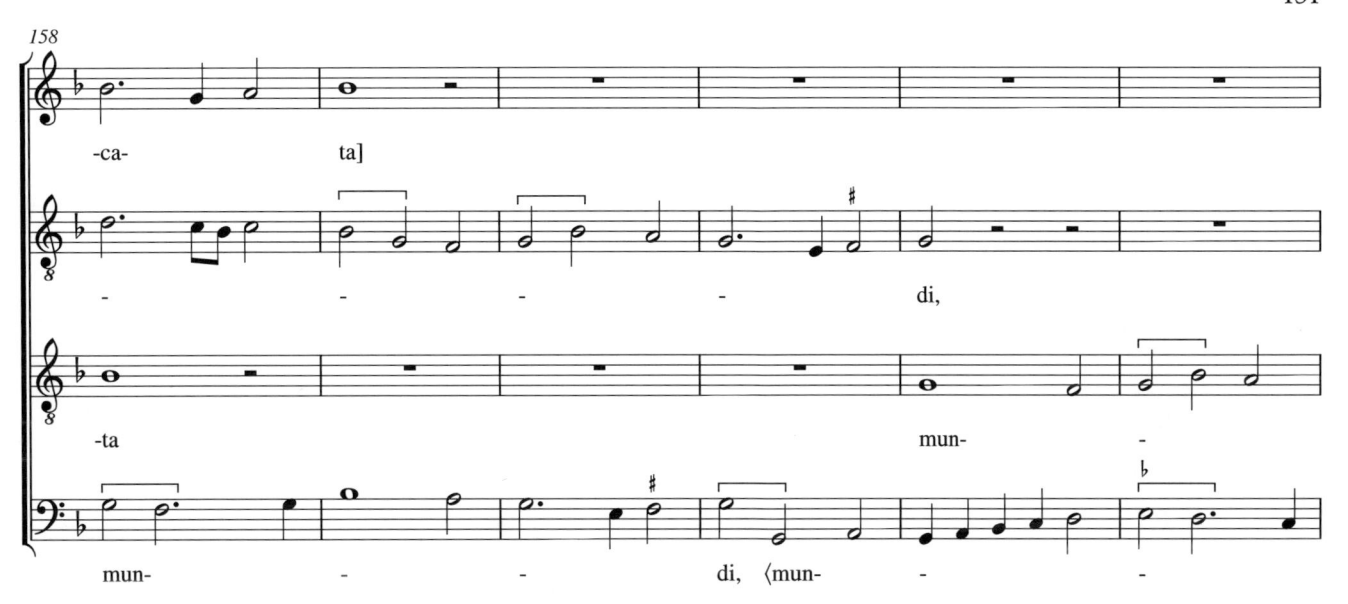

Missa Ma bouche rit

Kyrie

ModE M.1.13, no. 8

17
c
Chri- ste e- ley- - son, ⟨Chri- ste e- ley-
Chri- ste e- ley- son, ⟨Chri- ste e- ley-
Chri- ste e- ley- - son, ⟨Chri- ste e-
Chri- ste e- ley- son, ⟨Chri- - ste e- ley-
23
-son, Chri- ste e- ley- - son.⟩
- son, Chri- ste e- ley- son.⟩
-ley- son, Chri- ste e- ley- - son.⟩
- son, Chri- ste e- - ley- son.⟩
28
c
Ky- ri- e
Ky- ri- e e- ley- son, ⟨Ky-
Ky- ri- e e- ley-
Ky- ri- e e- ley- son, ⟨Ky- ri-

31
e- ley- son, ⟨Ky- ri-
-ri- e e- ley- son, Ky- ri-
-son, ⟨Ky- ri- e e- ley- son, Ky- ri-
-e e- ley- - son, Ky- ri-
34
-e e- ley- son, e- ley- son.⟩
-e e- - ley- son.⟩
-e e- ley- son.⟩
-e e- ley- - son.⟩

Gloria

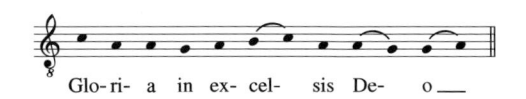

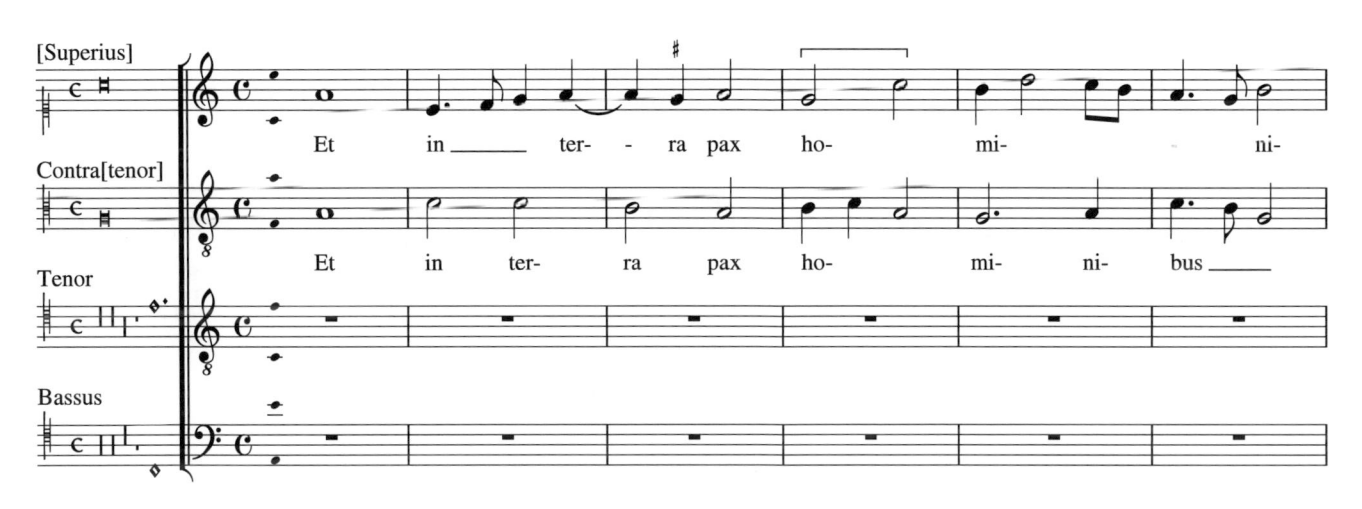

20
-mus te, glo- ri- fi- - ca- - mus te. Gra- ti- as a- gi- mus ti-
- mus te, [glo- ri- fi- ca- mus te.] Gra- ti- as a- gi- mus [ti-
[glo- ri- fi- - ca- mus te.] Gra- ti- as a- gi- mus ti-
te.] Gra- - ti- as a- gi- mus ti-
27
-bi pro- pter ma- - gnam glo- ri- am tu- - am.
-bi pro- pter ma- - gnam glo- ri- am tu- am.] Do- mi- ne De-
-bi [pro- - pter ma- gnam glo- ri- am tu- am.] Do- mi-
-bi pro- pter ma- gnam [glo- ri- am tu- - am.] Do- mi- ne [De-
33
De- us Pa- ter o- mni- po- tens. Do-
-us, De- - us Pa- ter o- mni- po-
-ne De- us, Rex cae- le- - stis,
-us, Rex cae- le- stis, De- us Pa- ter o- mni- po- tens.] Do-

157

158

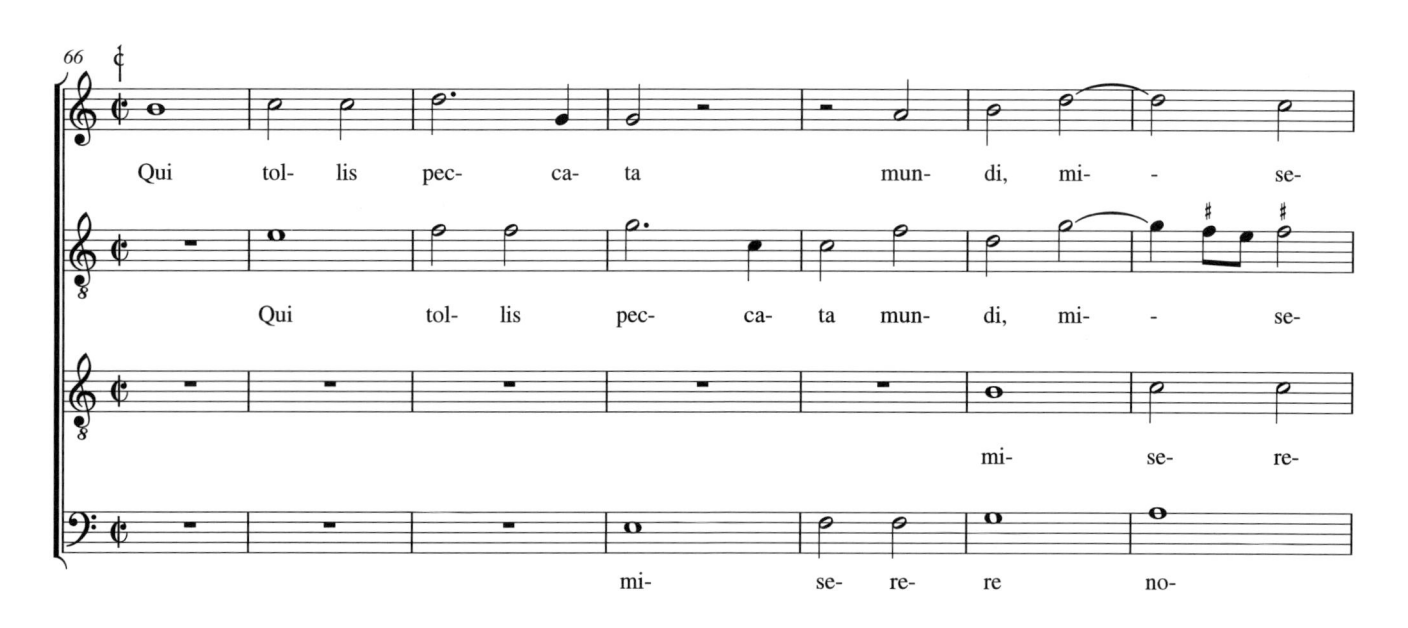

80
-ca- ta mun- di, su- sci- pe de- - pre- ca-
[pec- ca- ta mun- di,] su- sci- pe de- - pre- ca-
-ta mun- di,] su- - sci- pe de- pre- - ca- ti-
-ta mun- - di,] su- sci- pe de- pre- ca-
87
-ti- o- nem no- stram.
-ti- o- nem no- stram.
-o- nem no- - - -
-ti- o- - nem [no- - - -
93
Qui se- - des ad dex- - te- ram Pa- -
-stram. Qui se- - des ad dex- te- ram Pa- - tris,
-stram.]

99
-tris, tu
Quo- ni- am tu so- lus san- - ctus,
Quo- ni- am tu so- - lus [san- - ctus,] tu
105
so- lus Do- - mi- nus, tu so- lus al- tis- si- mus,
Je- -
so- lus [Do- - mi- nus, tu so- lus] al- tis- si- mus, Je- -
111
cum San- cto Spi-
cum San- cto Spi-
-su Chri- - - - ste:
-su Chri- - - - ste:

117
- - ri- tu, in glo- ri- a De- i Pa-
- ri- - tu, in glo- - ri- a [De- i
in glo- ri- a [De-
in glo- ri- a [De-
124
- tris. A- - - men.
Pa- tris.] A- - men.
-i Pa- tris. A- - - men.]
-i Pa- tris. A- - men.]

Credo

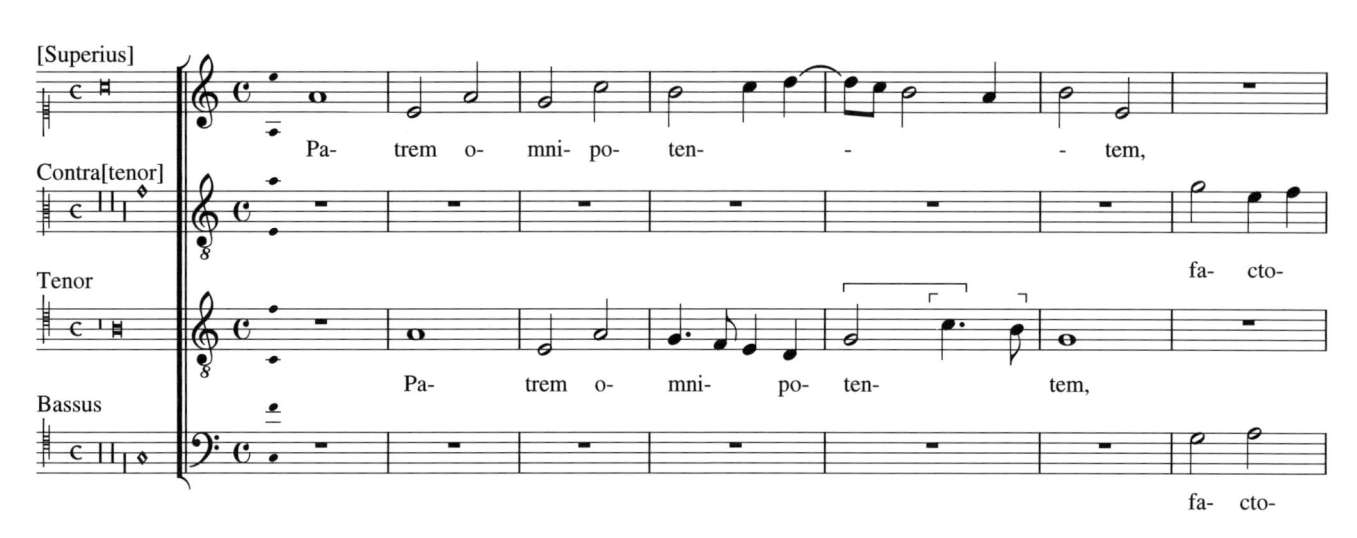

163

46
ge- ni- tum, non fa- - - ctum, con-sub- stan-
- rum [de De- o ve- - ro, non fa- ctum, con-
- o ve- - ro, ge- ni- tum, non fa- - ctum, con- sub- stan-
ve- rum de De- o ve- ro, ge- ni- tum, non fa- ctum, con-
53
- ti- - a- lem Pa- - - - tri,
-sub-stan- ti- a- lem Pa- tri,] per quem o- mni- a [fa- cta sunt.]
-ti- a- lem Pa- tri, per quem [o- mni- a fa- cta sunt.] Qui pro-pter
-sub-stan- ti- a- lem Pa- tri, per quem o- mni- a fa- cta sunt.] Qui pro-pter
60
et pro- pter no- stram sa- lu-
et pro- pter no- stram [sa- lu-
nos ho- - mi- nes, [et pro- pter no- - stram] sa- lu-
nos ho- mi- nes, et pro- - pter no-

66
-tem de- - scen- dit de cae- - lis.
- tem de- scen- dit de cae- - - lis.]
Tenor tacet
- tem [de- scen- dit de cae- - lis.]
- stram [sa- lu- tem de- scen- dit de cae- - lis.]
73
S
CT
B
Et in- car- na- - tus est de Spi- ri- tu San-
Et in- car- na- - tus est [de Spi- ri-
81
ex Ma- ri- a Vir- - gi-
- - cto
-tu San- - cto] ex Ma- ri- - a Vir-
87
- - ne, Cru- ci-
et ho- mo fa- - ctus est.
- gi- - ne, et ho- mo fa- ctus est. Cru- ci-

93
-fi- xus et- i- am pro no- - bis:
Cru- ci- fi- xus et- i- am pro no- bis: sub Pon- - ti- o Pi-
-fi- xus sub Pon- ti- - o Pi-
99
pas- sus, et se- pul- - tus
- la- to pas- sus, et se- pul- tus
-la- to et
104
est, [et re- sur- re- - xit,]
est, et re- sur- re- - xit ter- ti- a di-
re- sur- re- - xit [ter- ti- a di-
110
se- cun- - dum Scri- ptu- - ras, et a- scen-
- e, et a- scen- - dit
- e,] se- cun- - dum Scri- ptu- ras, et a- scen-

117
-dit in cae- - lum: se- - det ad
in cae- - lum: se- - det ad dex-
-dit in cae- lum: se- - det ad dex-
124
dex- te- ram Pa- - - tris.
- - te- ram Pa- - tris.
- te- ram Pa- - - tris.
130
S
CT
T
B
Et in Spi- ri- tum San- ctum, Do- -
Et in Spi- ri- tum San- - ctum, [Do-

136
- mi- num, et vi- - vi- fi- can- tem,
- mi- num, et vi- vi- fi- can- tem,
[et vi- - vi-
et vi- vi- fi- can-
143
qui ex Pa- tre Fi- - li- o-
qui ex Pa- - tre Fi- li-
-fi- - can- tem, qui ex
- tem, [Pa- tre Fi- li-
150
- que pro- ce- - dit. Qui cum Pa- - tre et Fi-
- o- que pro- ce- - dit. Qui cum Pa- tre et Fi-
Pa- tre
- o- que Qui cum Pa- tre et Fi-

169

178
et a- po- sto- - li- cam Ec-
-tho- - li- cam et a- po- sto- li- cam
- cle- - - - si-
a- po- sto- - li- cam
184
-cle- - si- am. Con- fi- te- or u- num ba- pti-
Ec- cle- si- am.] Con- fi- te- or [u- num ba- pti-
- - am] Con- fi te-
Ec- cle- - si- am.]
191
-sma in re- mis- si- o- nem pec-
-sma] in re- mis- si- o- nem pec- ca-
-or
Con- fi- - te- or [u- num ba- pti- sma

198
-ca- to- rum.
- to- rum. Et ex- spe- - -
in re- mis- si- o- nem pec- ca- to- rum.] Et ex- spe- -
204
3
Et vi- tam ven-
-cto re- - sur- re- cti- - o- nem mor- tu- - o- rum. Et vi- tam [ven-
Et vi- tam [ven-
-cto re- sur- re- cti- o- nem mor- tu- o- rum. [Et vi- tam ven-
211
-tu- - ri sae- cu- li. A- - men.
-tu- - ri sae- cu- - li A- men.]
-tu- - ri sae- cu- li. A- - men.]
-tu- - ri sae- cu- li. A- - men.]

Sanctus

173

40
- - - - - ba- oth.
Sa- - - - - ba- oth.]
Pleni tacet
Sa- - - - - ba- oth.]
Sa- - ba- - oth.]
46
c
S
CT
B
Ple- - ni sunt cae- -
Ple- ni sunt cae- - - -
52
- - li et ter- - - ra
- - li [et ter- - - ra
58
glo- - ri- a ⟨glo- - -
[glo- - ri- a, glo- - - ri-

175

78
- sis, ⟨in ex- cel- - sis,
- sis, in ex- cel- -
- sis, in ex- cel- - sis, in
- sis, in ex- cel- -
83
in ex- cel- sis, in ex- cel- - sis.⟩
- sis, in ex- - cel- - sis.]
ex- cel- sis, in ex- cel- sis, in ex- cel- sis.⟩
- sis, in ex- cel- - sis.]
88
Be- ne- di- - - - -
Be- - ne- - di- - ctus
Ben- ne-

95
- - ctus qui ve- nit
qui ve- - nit, (qui ve- nit)
[in
-di- - ctus qui [ve- - nit in
103
[in
[in no-
no- - mi- - ne Do- - - mi- ni.]
no- - mi- ne Do- - - - mi- ni.]
110
no- mi- ne] Do- - - mi- ni.
- - mi- ne] Do- - mi- ni.
[ni.]
[ni.]
[Osanna ut supra]
[Osanna ut supra]
[Osanna ut supra]
[Osanna ut supra]

Agnus Dei

179

37
S
CT
B
A- - - -
A- - - - gnus De-
42
-gnus De- - - i, qui
-i, ⟨De- - i,⟩ [qui
47
tol- - -
tol- - lis
52
-lis pec- - ca- ta mun- di,
pec- ca- - - - ta mun- - di,

181

Credo (Alternate Version)

Cre-do in u- num De-um

VerBC 761, fols. 56ᵛ–59

21
-num Do- - mi- num Je- sum Chri-stum, Fi- li- um De- i,
Do- mi- num Je- sum Chri- stum, Fi- li- um De- - i
u- num Do- mi- num Je- sum Chri- - stum,
-num Do- - mi- num Je- sum Chri- stum, Fi- - li- um De- i
28
et ex Pa- tre na- tum an-
u- ni- ge- ni- tum, et ex Pa- tre na- tum an-
[u- ni- ge- - ni- tum,] et ex Pa- tre na- tum an- te
u- ni- ge- - ni- tum, et ex Pa- tre na- tum an-
35
-te o- mni- a sae- - cu- la: lu- men de
-te o- mni- a sae- - cu- la:
o- mni- a sae- cu- la: De- um de De- - o,
-te o- mni- a sae- - cu la: De- um de De- o, lu- men de

42
lu- - mi- ne,
De- um ve- - rum de De- o
[de De- o ve- - ro,
lu- mi- ne, De- um ve- - rum de De- o
48
ge- ni- tum, non fa- ctum, con- sub- stan- - ti- a-
ve- ro, ge- ni- tum, non fa- ctum, con- sub- stan- ti-
ge- ni- tum, non fa- - ctum,] con- sub- stan- ti- a-
ve- ro, ge- ni- tum, non fa- ctum, con- sub- stan- ti- a-
54
- lem Pa- tri, per quem o- mni- a fa- - cta sunt.
-a- lem Pa- tri, per quem o- mni- a fa- cta sunt.
-lem Pa- tri, per quem o- mni- a fa- cta sunt. Qui pro- pter
-lem Pa- tri, per quem o- mni- a fa- cta sunt. Qui pro- pter

60
et pro-pter no- - stram sa- lu-
et pro-pter no- - stram sa- lu-
nos ho- mi- nes, et pro-pter no- - stram sa- lu-
nos ho- mi- nes, et pro- pter no-
66
-tem de- - scen- dit de cae- - lis.
-tem de- scen- dit de cae- - - lis.
Et incarnatus tacet
- tem de- - scen- - dit de cae- lis.
- stram sa- lu- tem de- scen-dit de cae- - lis.
73
S
A
B
Et in- car- na- - tus est de Spi-
Et in- car- na- - tus est de

80
ex Ma-
- ri- tu San- - cto
Spi- ri- tu San- cto ex Ma-
86
- ri- a Vir- - gi- ne,
et ho- mo fa- - ctus est.
-ri- a Vir- gi- ne, et ho- mo fa- ctus est.
92
Cru- ci- fi- xus et- i- am pro no- - bis:
Cru- ci- fi- xus et- i- am pro no- bis: sub Pon-
[Cru- ci- fi- xus] sub Pon- - ti-
98
pas- sus, et se- - pul- tus
- ti- o Pi- - la- to pas- sus, et se- - pul- tus
- o Pi- la- to et

104
est, ter- ti- a di- - e,
est, et re- sur- - re- xit, se- cun- dum Scri- ptu-
re- sur- re- - xit ter- ti- a di-
110
se- cun- - dum Scri- ptu- - ras. Et u-
- ras. Et u- nam san-
-e, se- cun- - dum Scri- - ptu- ras. Et
117
-nam san- - ctam et a- po-
- ctam ca- tho- li- cam et a- po-
u- nam san- ctam ca- tho- - li- cam et a- po-
123
-sto- li- cam Ec- - cle- - si- am.
-sto- - - li- cam Ec- - cle- - si- am.
-sto- - li- cam Ec- - cle- - si- am.

130
c
S
A
T
B
Con- fi- te- or u- num
Con- fi- te- or u- num
Con- fi- te- or u- num ba- - pti-
Con- fi- te- or u- num
138
ba- pti- sma in re- - mis- si- o- nem pec- - ca- to
ba- pti- sma in re- mis- si- o- nem pec-
- - - sma in re- mis- si-
in re- mis- si- o- - - nem pec-
145
rum. Et ex- spe- cto re- sur- rec- ti-
- ca- to- - rum. Et ex- spe- cto re-
- o- nem pec- - ca- to- rum. Et ex-
-ca- to- - rum. Et ex- spe- - cto

152
-o- nem mor- tu- o- rum, et
-sur- rec- ti- o- nem mor- tu- o- rum, et vi-
-spe- cto re- sur- rec- ti- o- nem mor- tu- o- rum, et
re- sur- rec- ti- o- - nem mor- tu- o- rum, et vi- - tam
158
vi- tam ven- tu- ri sae- - - cu-
- tam ven- - tu- - ri sae- - cu-
vi- tam ven- tu- ri sae- cu- - li.
ven- tu- - ri sae- - cu-
164
-li. A- - - men.
-li. A- - - men.
A- men, ⟨A- men, A- men, A- men.⟩
-li. A- - - men.

Missa Or sus, or sus
Kyrie

ModE M.1.13, no. 1

19
- - - ste ⟨e- ley- -
⟨e- ley- - - - -
⟨e-
⟨e-
26
- - - - son, Chri- -
-son, Chri- - - -
-ley- son, Chri- - ste⟩
-ley- - - - son,
32
-ste⟩ e-
-ste⟩ e- - - - ley-
e- ley- - - - son.
Chri- - ste⟩ e-

38
c
- ley- son. Ky- ri- e ⟨e- - ley-
- son. Ky- ri- e ⟨e-
Ky- ri- - e
- ley- son. Ky- ri- e
44
- - - son, Ky- ri- -
-ley- - son, Ky- ri- -
⟨e- ley- - son, Ky-
⟨e- ley- - - - - son, Ky-
50
- - e⟩ e- - - - ley- son.
-e⟩ e- - - - ley- son.
-ri- - e⟩ e- ley- - - son.
-ri- e⟩ e- - - - ley- son.

Gloria

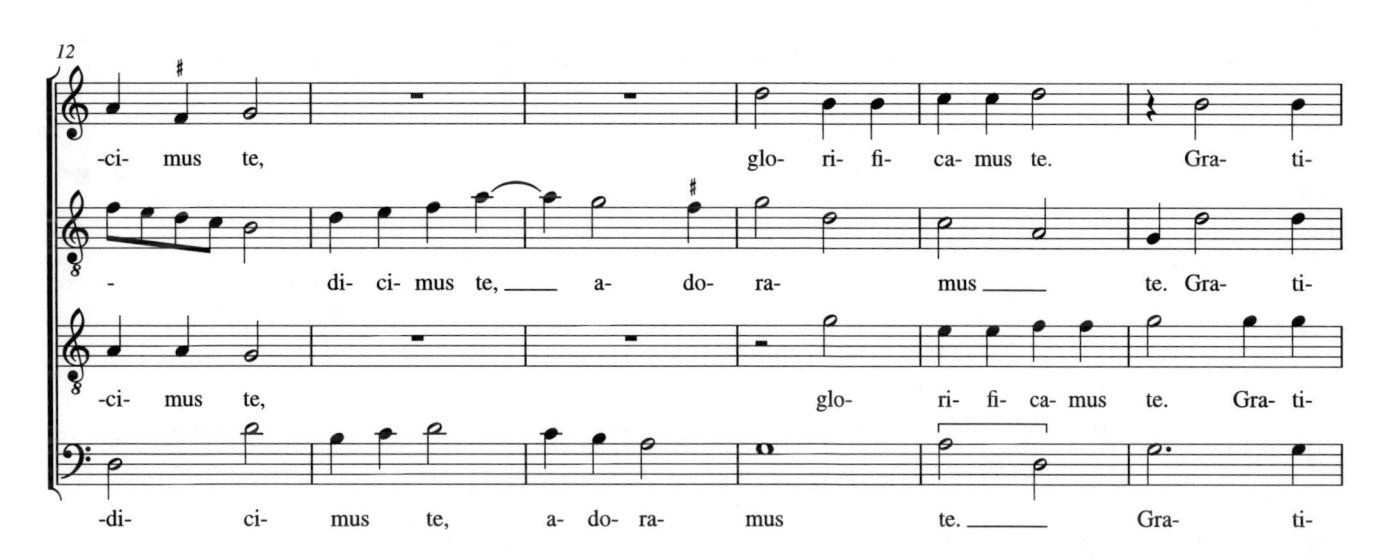

18
-as a- gi- - mus ti- bi pro- - pter ma- gnam [glo- ri- am
-as a- gi- mus ti- bi] pro- pter ma- gnam [glo- ri- am
-as a- gi- mus ti- bi [Do-
-as a- gi- mus ti- bi pro- pter ma- - gnam glo-
24
tu- am.] Do- mi- ne De- - us, Rex cae-
tu- am. Do- mi- ne De- us, Rex cae- le
-mi- ne De- us, Rex cae- le- - - -
-ri- am tu- am. Do- mi- ne De- - us, Rex cae- - le-
30
-le- stis, Do- mi- ne Fi- li
stis, De- us Pa- ter o- mni- - po- tens. Do- mi- ne Fi-
- stis,
-stis, De- us Pa- ter o- mni- - - po- tens. Do- - mi- ne

u- ni- ge- ni- te, Je- su Chri- ste. [Do- mi- ne
-li u- ni- ge- ni- te, Je- su Chri- ste.] Do- mi-
Fi-
Fi- li u- ni- ge- ni- te, Je- su Chri- ste. Do-

De- us, A- gnus De- i, Fi- li- us Pa- tris.]
-ne De- us, [Pa- tris.]
- li- us Pa- tris.]
-mi- ne De- us, A- gnus De- i, Fi- li- us Pa- tris.]

Qui tol- lis pec- ca- ta mun- di, mi- se- re-
Qui tol- lis pec- ca- ta
Qui tol- lis pec- ca- ta mun-
Qui tol- lis pec- ca- ta mun- di,

56
- re no- - - bis. Qui
mun- di, [qui tol-
- di, [mi- se- re- re no-
[mi- se- re- - re
62
tol- lis pec- ca- ta mun- - di, su- - sci- pe
-lis pec- ca- - ta mun- di, su- - sci-
- - - bis.]
no- - - - bis.
68
de- pre- ca- ti- - o- nem no- - stram.
-pe de- pre- ca- - ti- o- - nem no- stram. Qui se- des
Qui
Qui tol- lis pec- ca- ta mun-

74
Qui se- des ad dex- te- ram Pa- tris,
ad] dex- te- ram Pa- tris,
se- des [ad dex- te- ram Pa- tris,
- - - di,
80
mi- se- re- re no- - -
[mi- se- re- re, no- - - bis.]
mi- se- re-
mi- se re- re no- bis.]
86
- bis. Quo- ni- am tu so-
Quo- ni- am tu so- - -
- re

92
- lus san- - ctus,
- lus san- - ctus, tu so- lus Do- mi- -
tu so- lus al- - tis- si-
98
tu so- lus al- tis
- - - nus, tu so- lus
tu
- mus, Je- su
103
si- mus, Je- su
al- - tis- si- - mus, Je- - - su Chri-
so- - lus
Chri- - - ste,

Chri- - ste
- ste, ⟨Je- - - su Chri-
al- tis- - si- mus, Je- su Chri-
⟨Je- su Chri-
cum San- - - - cto
-ste:⟩ cum San- - - - cto
-ste:] cum San- - cto
-ste:⟩ cum San- - cto
Spi- ri- -
Spi- - ri- - tu, ⟨cum San- - cto
[Spi- ri- tu,
[Spi- ri- - - - - -

126
- tu in glo- ri- a De-
Spi- ri- tu,〉 [in glo- ri- a De- - - -
in glo- ri- a De-
-tu, in glo- ri- a
133
-i Pa- - - - tris.
- i Pa- - tris. A- -
- i Pa- - -
De- i Pa- - tris, De- - i Pa- tris.
140
A- - - - men.
- - men, A- - - men.]
- tris. A- men, A- - men.]
A- men, A- - men.]

Credo

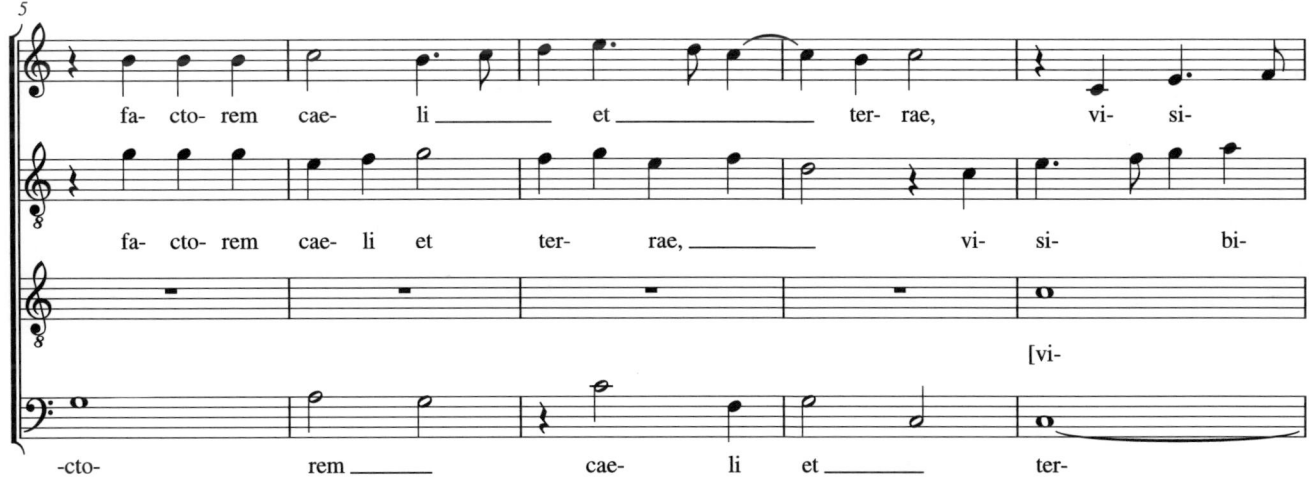

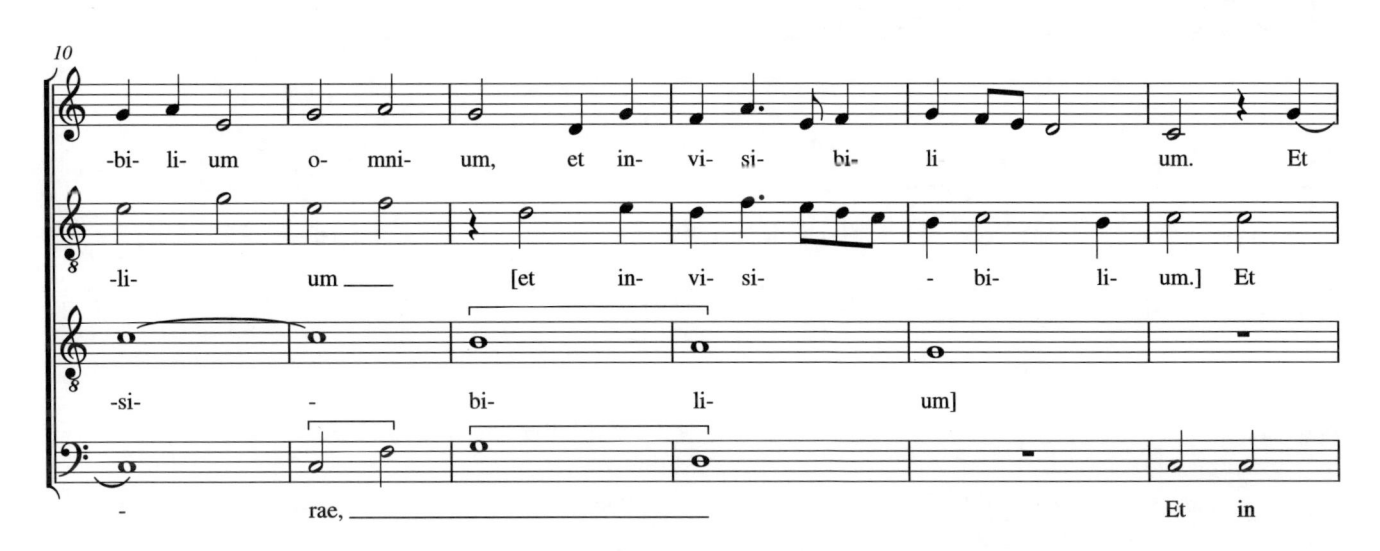

16
in u- num Do- mi- num Je- sum Chri- stum, Fi- li- um De- - i
in u- num Do- mi- num [Je- sum Chri- stum, Fi- li- um De- i u-
Je- - sum Chri-stum, [Fi- li- um
u- num Do- - mi- num Je- sum Chri- - stum, Fi-
22
u- ni- - ge- ni- tum, et ex Pa- tre na- tum an- te o- mni- a sae-
-ni- ge- ni- tum,] et ex Pa- tre na- tum [an- te o- mni- a
De- - i] et ex Pa- tre na- tum [an- te o- mni- a
-li- um De- i et ex Pa- tre na- tum an- te o-
28
- cu- la: lu- men de lu- mi- ne,
sae- cu- la:] De- um de De- - o, lu- men de lu-
sae- cu- la:]
- mni- a sae- cu- la: De- um de De- o, [lu- men de lu- mi-

34
De- um ve- rum de De- o ve- ro, ge- ni- tum,
-mi- ne, De- um ve- rum de De- o ve- ro, ge- ni-
-ne,] De- - um ve- - rum [de De- o ve- ro, ge-
40
non fa- ctum, con- sub- stan- ti- a- lem Pa- tri, per quem o- mni- a
-tum, non fa- ctum, [con- sub- stan- ti- a- lem Pa- tri,]
con- sub- stan- - ti- a- - lem Pa- tri, [per quem o- mni-
-ni- tum, non fa- ctum, con- sub- stan- ti- a-
46
fa- cta sunt. Qui pro- pter nos ho- mi- nes, de-
Qui pro- pter nos ho- mi- nes, et pro- pter no- stram sa- lu-
-a fac- ta sunt.] et pro- pter no- stram sa- lu- tem
-lem Pa- - tri, et pro- pter no- stram sa-

51
- scen- - dit de cae- - lis.
-tem de- scen- dit [de cae- - - lis.]
[Tenor tacet]
de- - scen- dit de cae- lis.
-lu- tem de- scen- - dit de cae- - lis.]
57
[S]
Et in- - car- na- - tus est
CT
Et in- car- na- tus est
B
64
de Spi- - - - ri-
de Spi- - - -

69
- tu San- - - cto ex
- ri- tu San- - - cto
ex Ma-
75
Ma- - ri- - a Vir- gi- -
ex Ma- ri- - a Vir-
- ri- - - a Vir- gi- ne,
81
- ne, et ho- mo
-gi- ne, et ho- - mo fa-
[et ho- - -
87
fa- ctus est.
- - - - ctus est.
-mo fa- - ctus est.]

[S]: Cru- ci- fi- xus et- i- am pro no- - - bis: sub Pon- ti- -o Pi- la- to pas- sus, et se- pul- tus

CT: Cru- ci- fi- xus et- i- am [pro no- - bis:] sub Pon- ti- o Pi- la- -to pas- sus, et se- pul- tus

T: Cru- ci- fi- xus et- i- am [pro no- - bis:]

B: Cru- ci- fi- xus [et- -i- am pro no- - bis: sub Pon- ti- o Pi- la- to

113
est, et re- - sur- re- xit ter- - ti- a di- e, se-
est, et re- - sur- re- xit ter- - ti- a di- e, se-
et re- - sur- re- xit ter- - ti- a di- e, se-
et re- - sur- re- xit ter- - ti- a di- e, se-
121
-cun- dum Scri- ptu- ras, et a- scen- dit in cae- lum:
-cun- dum Scri- ptu- ras, [et a- scen- dit in cae- lum:
-cun- dum Scri- ptu- ras, et a- scen- dit in cae- lum:
-cun- dum Scri- ptu- ras, et a- scen- dit in cae- lum:
128
se- det ad dex- te- ram Pa- - -
se- det] ad dex- te- ram Pa- - -

134
-tris. Et i- - te- rum ven- tu- rus est cum
-tris. [Et i- te- - rum ven- tu- - - rus est
Et i- te- rum ven- tu- rus est [cum
Et i- te- rum ven- tu- rus est cum
141
glo- ri- - a, ju- di- - ca- - re
cum glo- ri- a, ju- di- ca-
glo- ri- - - -
glo- ri- - a, ju- - di- ca- -
147
vi- vos et mor- tu-
-re vi- - - vos]
-a]
-re vi- vos et mor- tu-

153
- os:
cu- jus re- - - gni
- - os: cu- jus re-
159
cu- jus re- gni non e- rit
[non e- rit fi- nis, non e- - rit fi-
-gni,
165
fi- nis.
-nis.]
non e- - rit fi- nis.
cu- - jus re- gni non e- rit fi- -

171
Et in Spi- ri- tum San- ctum, Do- - mi-
Et in Spi- ri- tum San- ctum, [Do- mi-
Et in Spi- ri- tum [San- ctum,
-nis.] Et in Spi- ri- tum [San-
177
-num, et vi- vi- fi- can- - - -
-num, et vi- vi- fi- can- - tem,
et vi- vi- fi- can-
-ctum, et vi-
183
- tem, qui ex Pa- tre Fi- li- o-
qui ex Pa- tre Fi- li- o- que pro- ce-
-tem qui ex Pa-
- vi- fi- can- tem, qui ex Pa- tre Fi- li-

189
-que pro- ce- dit. Con- fi- te- or u-
-dit. Con- fi- te- or u-
-tre ba-
-o- que pro- ce- dit. Con- fi- te- -
195
-num ba- pti- - sma in re- mis- si-
-num ba- ptis- - ma in re- mis- si-
- ptis- ma] in re- mis- si-
-or u- num ba- pti- sma in re- mis- si-
201
-o- nem pec- ca- to- rum.
-o- nem pec- ca- to- rum.
-o- nem Et ex- spe- cto re- sur- re- cti-
-o- - nem pec- ca- to- rum. Et ex- spe-

208
et vi- - - tam ven-
et vi- - tam
-o- nem et vi- tam ven- tu-
-cto et vi- tam ven-
214
-tu- - ri sae- cu- - li.
ven- tu- ri sae- cu- li.
- ri sae- cu- li.
-tu- ri sae- cu- li.
220
A- - - men.
A- - - - men.]
⟨A- men,⟩ A- - - men.
A- - - - men.]

Sanctus

214

215

52
in
-san- na [in ex- cel-
57
⟨ex- - cel- sis, in⟩ ex- cel-
[in
- - - sis, in ex- cel-
62
- - - - sis.
ex- cel- - - sis.]
[tacet]
- - - - sis.]
67
Duo
[S]
Be- ne- di- - - - -
CT
Be- ne- di- - -
74
- - ctus, ⟨be- ne- - di- - ctus⟩
- - ctus, ⟨be- ne- - di- - - ctus⟩

80
qui ve- - - - -
qui ve- - -
86
- - nit in no- mi- -
- - nit in no- mi- - -
92
- ne, ⟨in no- mi- - ne Do- mi-
- ne, ⟨in no- mi- - ne⟩ Do- mi- - ni,
99
- ni, Do- mi- ni, in no- mi- -
⟨Do- mi- ni, in no- mi- - - ne
105
- ne⟩ Do- mi- - - ni.
Do- mi- - - ni.⟩

111
[S]
CT
T
B
O- - san- na,
O- - - san- na, ⟨O-
O- - san-
O- - san- - na, ⟨O-
117
⟨O- san- na⟩
-san- - - na⟩
-na, ⟨O- san-
-san- na, O- san- na⟩
123
in ex- cel- - - -
[in ex- cel-
-na⟩ [in ex- cel- -
[in ex- cel- - - -

219

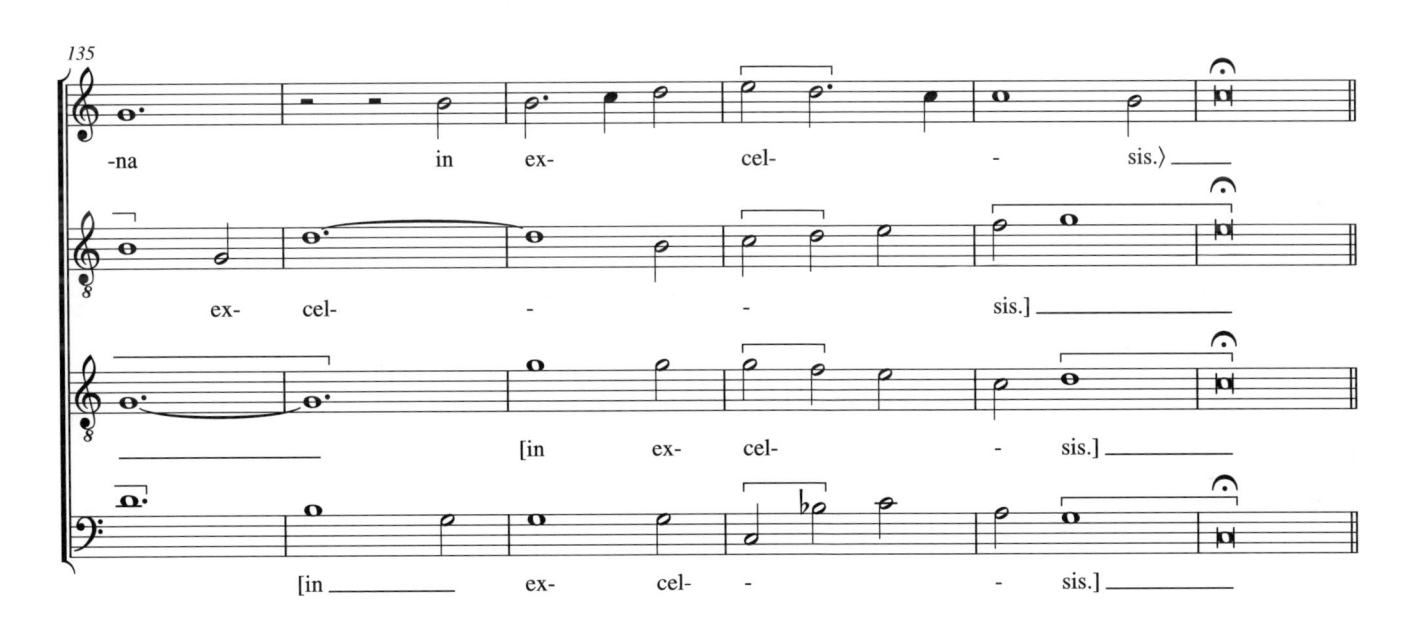

Agnus Dei

17
- ta mun- - - -
- ta mun- - - -
- ta mun- - -
[Quar on- que tiel oye- seau ne fut,
22
3
c
-di, mi- se- re- re
-di, mi- se- - re- -
-di, mi- se- re- -
"Je- - nin, Je-
27
no- - - - - bis.
- - re no- - bis.]
- - re no- - bis.]
Agnus 2us tacet
-not, es- tu point ma- ri- é? -é?]

33
[S]
CT
T
A- - gnus De- i, qui
A- - gnus De- i,
39
tol- - lis pec-
qui ⟨tol- - -
44
- ca- ta mun- - -
- - - lis, qui⟩ tol-
50
- - - di,
- - - lis pec- - ca-
qui tol-

56
-ta mun- - di, mi- se-
- - lis pec- ca- - ta
61
mi- se- re- re
- re- - re, ⟨mi- se-
mun- - di, mi- se- re-
66
⟨no- - - -
- re- - - -
- re, ⟨mi- se- - re- - re⟩
71
-bis,⟩ no- - - bis.
- - re⟩ no- - - bis.
no- - - - - bis.

224

Sheet music.

Lyrics by voice:

Voice 1 (m. 93+): pec- ca- -di, A- gnus De- i,] qui tol- - lis -ta mun- - - di,] ⟨A- gnus

Voice 2: -di, A- gnus De- - i,] qui tol- - lis [pec- ca- - ta mun- - di, A- gnus De-

Voice 3: [qui tol- lis pec- ca- ta, pec- ca- ta mun- di, ⟨A- - gnus

Bass: si- re que Dieux en ait bon gré, [a u- ne

110
De- - i, qui tol- - lis
- - i,] qui tol- - lis
De- i,⟩ [qui tol- - - - - lis
fil- lee qui d'a- mer
116
pec- ca- - - - -
[pec- ca- - - - -
pec- ca- - - - -
121
- ta mun- - -
- ta mun-
-ta mun- - -
m'a pri-

125
- - - di,⟩
- - di, do- na no-
- di, do- - -
- é. "Je- nin
130
do- na no-
- bis pa- cem, do- na no-
- na no- - bis
Je- not, es- tu point
135
- - - bis pa- cem.
- bis pa- - cem.]
pa- - - - cem.]
ma- rié?]

Missa Nos amis

Kyrie

ModE M.1.13, no. 4 (Anonymous)

12
e- ley- son. Chri- - -
- son,⟩ e- - ley- son. Chri- - -
-ley- - son.
e- ley- - son. Chri- ste
18
-ste ⟨e- ley- - -
-ste ⟨e- ley- - -
⟨e- ley- - - son,
23
-son, Chri- - - ste e- -
-son, Chri- -
Chri- -
Chri- - - - ste

230

46
- ste⟩ e- ley- - son.
- ste⟩ e- ley- - son.
-son,⟩ e- ley- - - son.
-son,⟩ e- ley- - son
51
Ky- ri- e ⟨e- - ley- - son,
Ky- ri- e ⟨e- ley- - - son, Ky-
Ky- ri- e ⟨e- - ley- son, Ky-
Ky- ri- e ⟨e- - ley- - son, Ky-
55
Ky- ri- e e- ley-
-ri- - e e- - ley-
-ri- - e e-
- ri- e e- ley- son, Ky- ri-

59
- son, Ky- ri- e e-
- son, Ky- ri- e e- ley- son,
-ley- son, Ky- ri- e⟩
-e e- ley- - son, Ky- ri-
63
- ley- - son,⟩ e- ley- son.
Ky- ri- - e e- ley- - son,⟩ e- ley- son.
e- ley- - - son.
- e e- ley- son,⟩ e- ley- son.

Gloria

12
-ci- mus te, a- do- ra- mus te, glo- ri-
-ci- mus te,] a- do- ra- mus te, [glo- ri- fi-
-mus glo- ri- fi-
a- do- ra- mus te, glo- ri- -
16
-fi- ca- - mus te. Gra- ti- as a- gi- mus
-ca- mus te.] Gra- - ti- as a- gi-
-ca- - mus te. Gra- ti- as a- gi- mus
-fi- ca- - mus te. Gra- ti- as a- gi-
20
ti- bi, ⟨a- gi- mus ti- bi⟩ pro- pter ma-
-mus [ti- bi
ti- - bi pro- pter ma- gnam
-mus ti- bi pro-

24
-gnam glo- ri- am tu- am. Do- mi- ne De-
pro- pter ma- gnam glo- ri- am tu- am.] Do- mi- ne De-
glo- ri- am tu- am.] Do- mi-
- pter ma- gnam glo- ri- am tu- am.]
28
-us, Rex cae- le- - stis, De- us Pa-
- us, [Rex cae- le stis, De- us
-ne De- us,
Do- mi- ne De- us, [Rex cae- le- stis,
32
-ter o- mni- po- tens. Do- mi- ne
Pa- ter o- mni- po- tens. Do- mi-
De- us Pa- ter o- mni- po- tens. Do- mi-

35
Fi- li u- ni- - ge- ni- te,
- ne Fi- li u- - ni- ge-
[Do- mi- ne Fi- li u-
- ne Fi- li u- - ni- ge-
38
⟨u- ni⟩- ge- ni- - te, Je-
- ni- te, Je- - -
-ni- ge- ni- - te, Je-
- ni- te, Je- -
42
-su Chri- - ste.
-su Chri- - - ste. ste.]
-su Chri- ste.]
-su Chri- - ste.]

46
Do- mi- ne De- us, A- gnus De-
Do- - mi- ne De- us, [A- -
Do- - - - mi- - ne
Do- - mi- - ne De- - us,
52
- i, Fi- - li- us Pa-
- gnus De- i, Fi- li- - us Pa-
De- us,
[A- gnus De- - i, Fi- li-
58
- - tris. Qui tol- - lis pec-
- - tris. Qui tol- -
[Qui
- us Pa- tris. Qui tol- - - lis

64
-ca- - ta mun- - di, mi- se- - -
- - - lis pec- ca- ta
tol- - - lis
pec- ca- ta mun- - -
72
-re- re no- - - - bis.
mun- di, mi- se-
mi-
-di, mi- se- - re- re
79
Qui tol- -
- re- re no- - bis. Qui
- se- re- re no- -
no- bis. Qui tol- -

86
-lis pec- ca- - -
tol- - lis pec- ca- - ta,
-bis.
- - lis pec- - ca- -
94
- - ta mun-
pec- ca- - - - ta
pec- - ca- - ta
-ta mun- - - - -
101
- di, su- - sci- - -
mun- - - - - di, su-
mun- - di, su- sci-
- di, su- sci-

108
- - pe
- sci- pe, su- sci- - pe de- -
-pe
- pe de- - pre- - ca- -
116
de- pre- ca- ti- o- nem no- - stram. Qui
-pre- - ca- - ti- - - o- nem no-
de- pre- ca- ti- - o- nem
-ti- - o- nem no- - stram. Qui
124
se- des ad
-stram. Qui se- des ad
no- - stram. Qui se- des
se- - - des ad dex-

132
dex- - - te- - ram Pa-
dex- te- - ram Pa- -
ad dex- te- ram
- te- - ram Pa- -
139
- - - - tris, mi-
- tris, mi- - se- - re- -
Pa- - tris, mi- - -
- - - tris, mi- - se- re-
146
-se- re- re no- - bis.
-re no- - - bis.]
-se- re- - re no- bis.]
-re no- - - bis.]

153
o 3
Quo- ni- am tu so- lus
Quo- ni- - - - am
Quo- ni- am tu so- lus [san-
Quo- ni- am tu so- lus
159
san- ctus, tu so- lus Do- mi- nus,
tu so- lus San- - ctus,
-ctus
san- ctus, [tu so- - lus Do- -
165
tu so- lus al-
tu so- lus al- tis- si- mus,
al- tis- - si- - mus,
-mi- nus, tu so- - lus al-

243

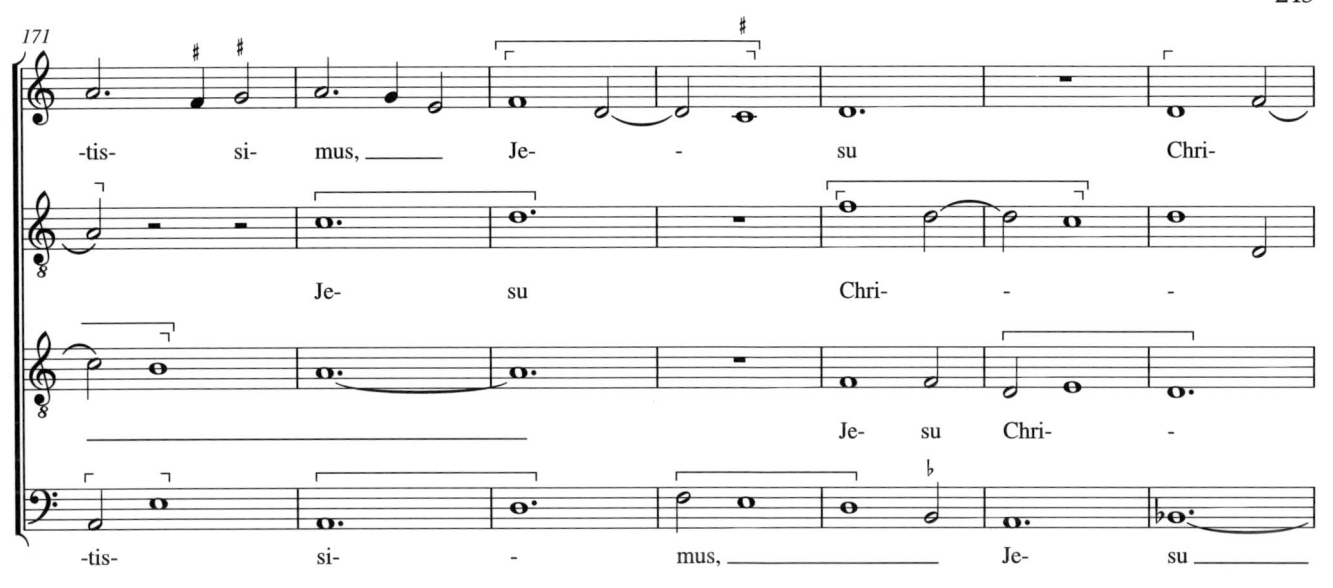

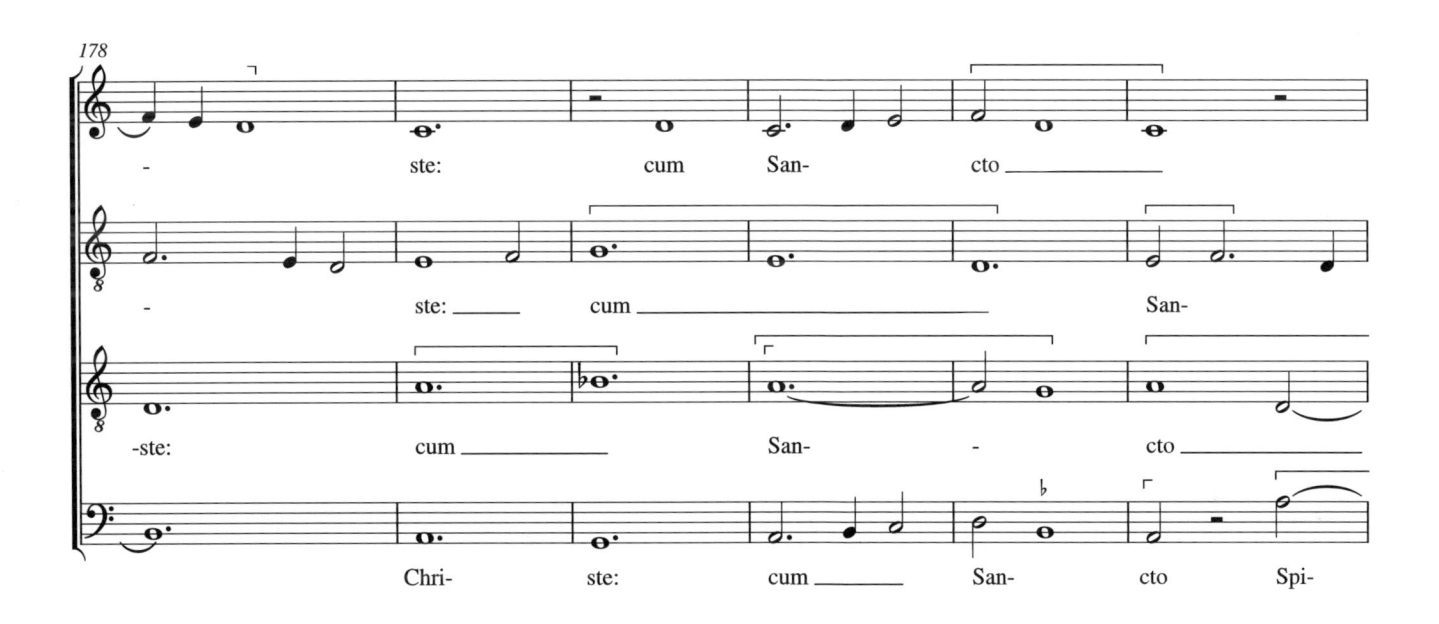

244

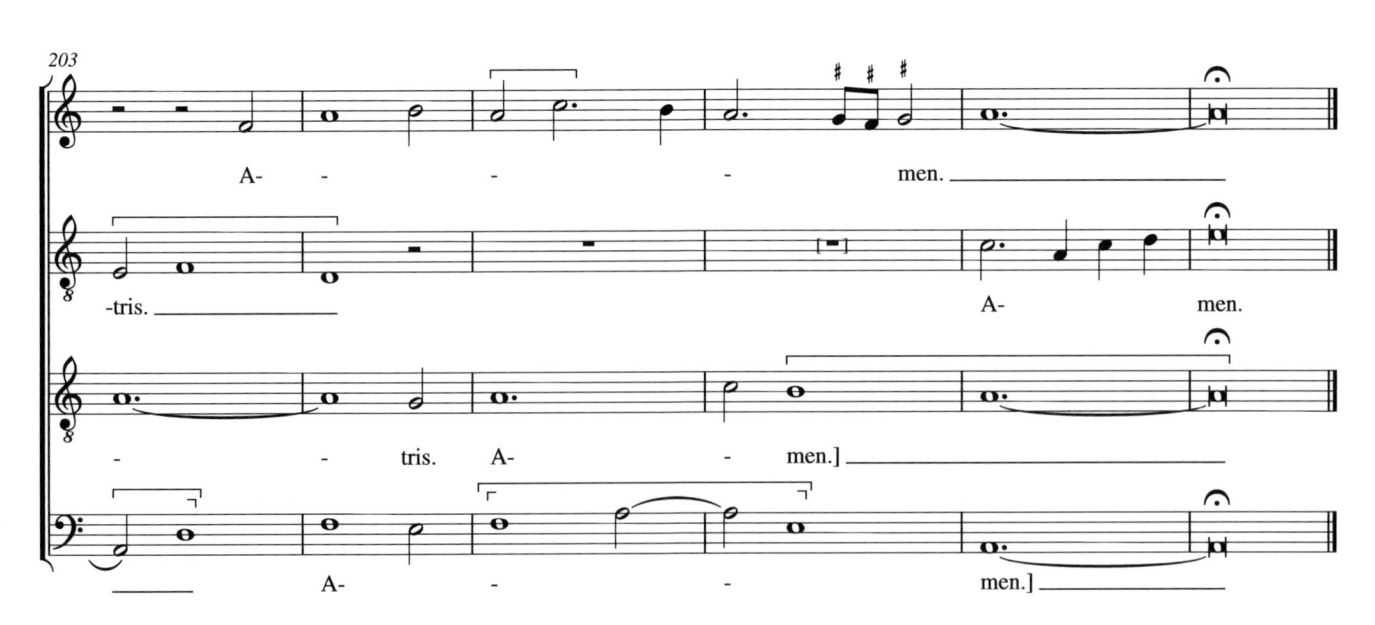

Credo

246

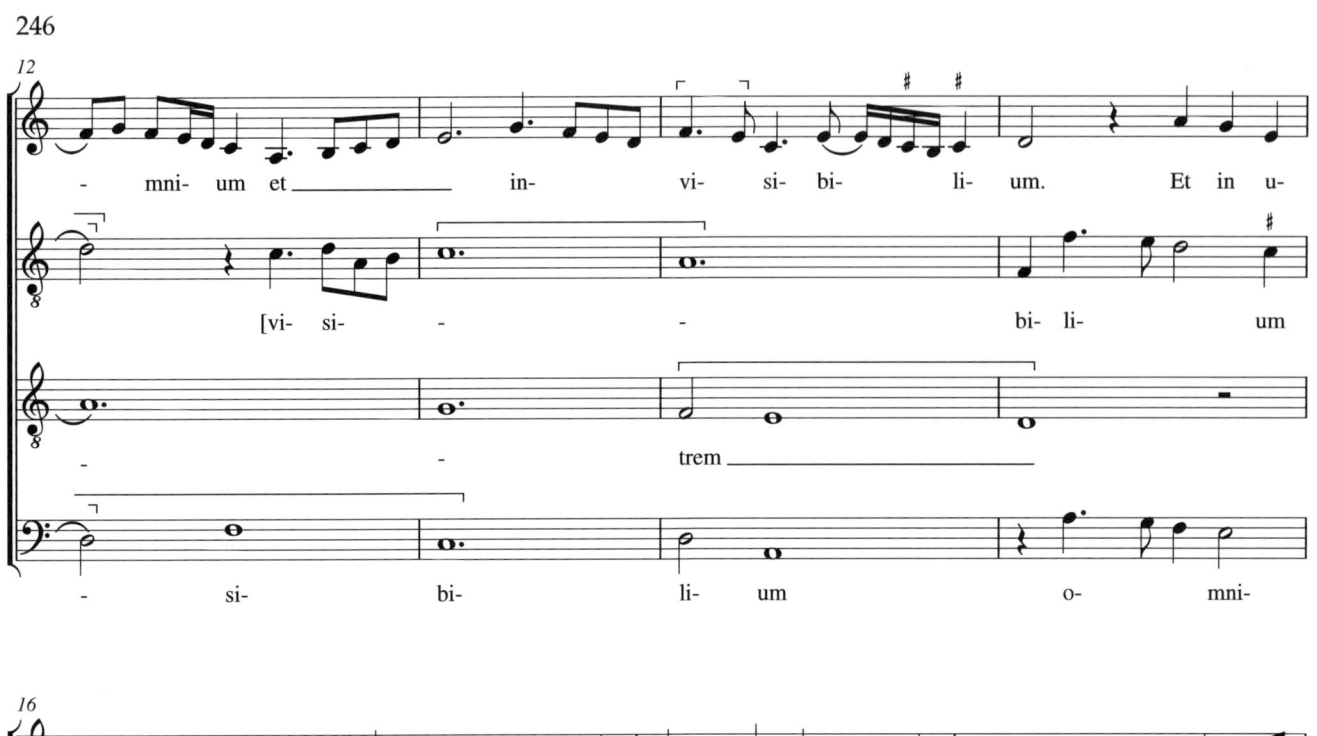

24
Pa- tre
na- tum an- te o- mni-
-i u- - ni- ge- ni- tum,]
Do- mi- - num Je- sum Chri- -
-tum,] et ex Pa- - tre
28
-a sae- - cu- - la: De-
et ex Pa- tre na- - tum [an- te o-
-stum, De-
na- - tum [an- te
32
- um de De- o, lu- men de lu- mi-
-mni- a- sae- cu- la: lu- men- de
- um ve- rum de De- o ve-
o- - mni- a sae- cu- la: De- um

36
-ne, ge- ni- tum, non fa- - ctum,
lu- mi- ne,] De- um ve- rum de De- o ve- ro,
-ro, ge- ni- tum, non fa- ctum, con- sub-
ve- rum de De- o ve- ro, ge-
41
con- sub- stan- ti- a- lem Pa- tri, per quem
[con- sub- - stan- ti- - a- lem Pa- tri,
-stan- ti- a- lem per quem o-
-ni- tum, non fa- ctum, con- - sub- stan- ti- a- lem Pa-
46
o- mni- a fa- cta sunt.
per quem o- mni- a fa- cta sunt.]
-mni- a fa- - cta sunt.]
-tri, per quem o- mni- a fa- cta sunt.]

249

72
ho- mo fa- - - ctus
-ne,⟩ et ho- - mo fa- ctus
Vir- - gi- ne, et
ho- - mo fa- - ctus
80
est. Cru- ci- fi- xus et- i- am
est. Cru- - ci- fi- - xus
ho- mo fa- ctus est. [Cru- - ci- fi
est. [Cru- - ci- fi
87
pro no- bis: sub Pon- ti- - o Pi- la- to
[sub Pon- ti- - o Pi- -
xus
xus et- i- - am pro no- bis:] Et

94
pas- sus, et se- pul- - tus est.
-la- to pas- sus, et se- pul-
se- - pul-
i- te- - rum ven- - tu- rus
101
Et in
- tus est, et a- - scen- dit in cae- - lum:
-tus est. Et in Spi-
est [cum glo- - ri- a, ju- di-
108
Spi- ri- - tum San- - ctum, Do- mi-
se- det ad dex- - te- ram Pa- -
- ri- tum San- - ctum,]
- ca- re] vi- vos

115
-num, et vi- vi- - fi- can- - tem, qui ex Pa-
- - tris.]
Fi- - li-
et mor- - tu- - os [cu- -
122
- tre Fi- li- o- que pro- ce- - dit.
Et i- te- rum ven- -
- o- - que
-jus re- - gni
129
si- mul a- - do-
-tu- - rus est [cum glo- ri- - a, ju- - di-
Qui [cum Pa- tre et Fi- - li- o si- mul
non e- - - rit fi- - -

137
-ra- tur, et con- glo- ri- - fi- - ca- tur:
-ca- re vi- vos et] mor- tu- os: cu- jus re-
a- - do ra- - tur,]
-nis, cu- - - jus re- - gni
145
qui lo- cu- tus est per pro- phe- -
-gni [non e- rit fi- nis.] Con- fi-
Con- - fi- te- or [u- num
non e- rit fi- nis.] Con- fi- -
152
-tas. in
-te- or u- num ba- pti- sma in
ba- - - pti- sma]
-te- or u- - num ba- pti- sma in re-

158
re- mis- si- o- nem pec- ca- - to- rum.
re- mis- si- o- nem [pec- ca- to-
in re- - -
-mis- si- o- nem [pec- ca- to- rum. Et
163
Et ex- spe- -
- rum. Et ex- spe- cto re- sur- re-
-mis- si- o- - nem
ex- - spe- - cto re- sur-
168
-cto re- sur- re- cti- o- nem mor- tu-
-cti- o- nem
[pec- - ca- to- - rum, pec- ca- to-
- - re- cti- - o- nem mor- tu-

174
- o- rum,
et vi- tam ven- tu- ri
-rum. Et vi-
-o- rum, et vi- - tam ven- tu-
179
et vi- tam ven- tu- ri sae- cu-
sae- cu- - li. A- - -
- tam ven- tu- ri sae-
-ri sae- - cu- li.
185
-li. A- - - - - men.
- - - men, A- men.]
-cu- li. A- - - - men.]
A- - - - men.

Sanctus

257

258

259

76
-cel- - sis,⟩ in ⟨ex- cel-
-cel- sis,] ⟨O- san- - na⟩
⟨O- san- na, O-
⟨O- san- - na⟩ [in ex-
82
- sis, O- san- -
[in ex- - cel- sis,]
- san- - - - na⟩ [in ex- cel-
- cel- - - sis,] ⟨O- san- na⟩
89
-na in ex- cel- sis, O- san-
⟨O- - san- na⟩ [in ex- -
-sis,] ⟨O- san-
[in ex- - -

96
- na in ex- cel-
-cel- - - - sis,]
-na⟩ [in ex- cel-
-cel- - sis, in ex- -
102
-sis, O- - san- -
⟨O- - san- - na⟩ [in
-sis,] ⟨O- san-
-cel- - - sis,] ⟨O-
108
-na in⟩ ex- - cel- sis.
ex- cel- - sis, in ex- cel- sis.]
[Benedictus tacet]
- na⟩ [in ex- cel- - sis.]
[Benedictus tacet]
-san- - - na⟩ [in ex- cel- sis.]

262

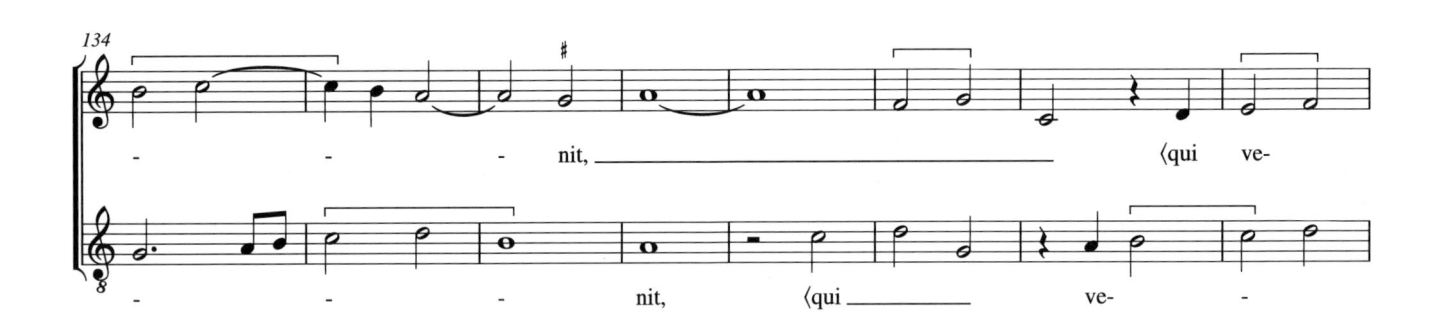

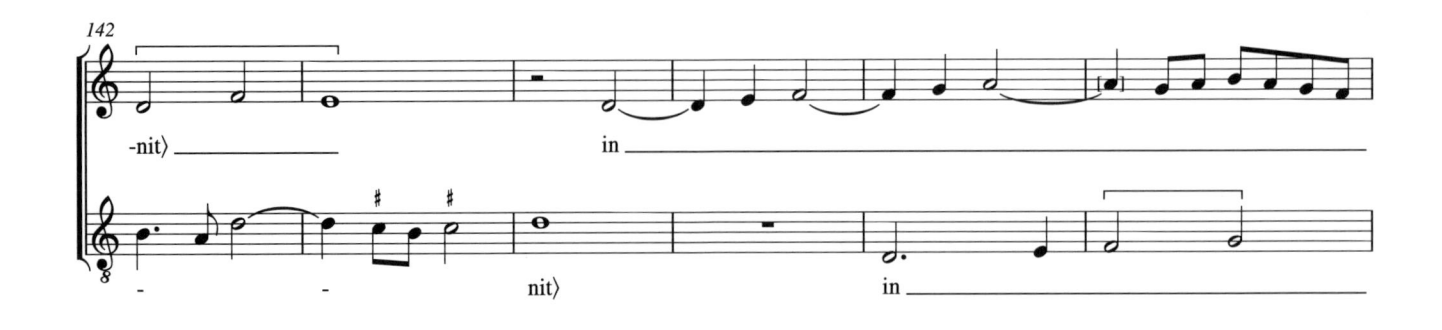

263

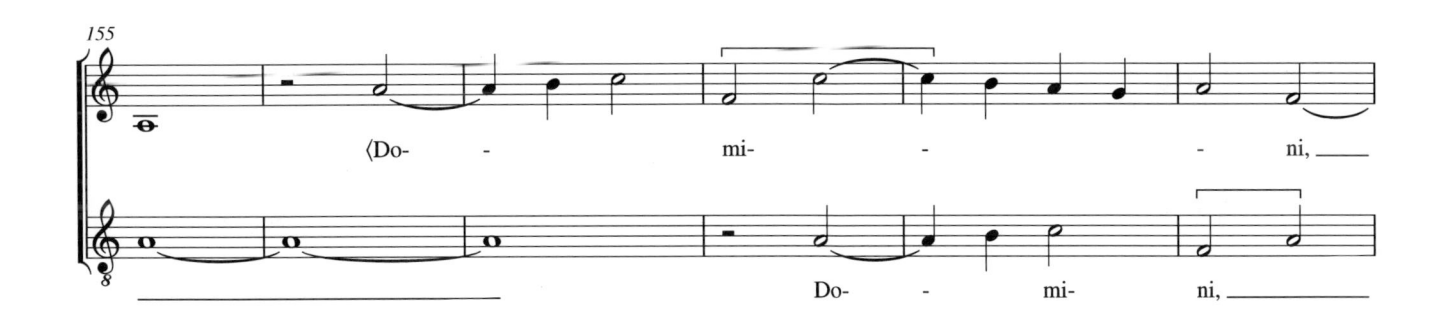

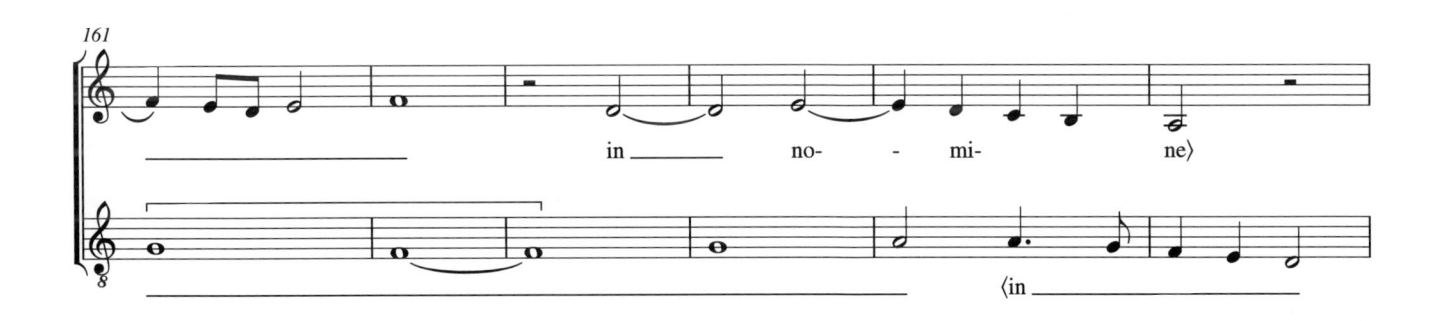

Agnus Dei

265

no- - - bis.
pa- - - cem.
-re- - re nobis.]
no- - bis pa- cem.]
[Agnus 2us tacet]
no- - - bis.]
pa- - - cem.]
[Agnus 2us tacet]
no- bis, no- - bis.]
pa- cem, pa- - cem.]
S
A- - gnus De-
CT
A- - gnus De-
- - - i, qui
- - i, qui
tol- - - - lis
tol- -

50
pec- - ca- - - - -
-lis pec- ca- -
57
- - ta mun- - - - -
- - - ta mun- - - - -
65
- di, mi- se- - - re-
- - - - di, mi- se- -
73
-re, ⟨mi- se- - - re- - re⟩
- re- re, ⟨mi- se- - re- - re⟩
80
no- - - bis.
[Agnus ut supra]
no- - - - - bis.
[Agnus ut supra]

Critical Report

List of Sigla and Abbreviations

The sigla and abbreviations in this edition are taken from Charles Hamm and Herbert Kellman, eds., *The Census-Catalogue of Manuscript Sources of Polyphonic Music, 1400–1550, Compiled by the University of Illinois Musicological Archives for Renaissance Manuscript Studies*, 5 vols. (Neuhausen-Stuttgart: Hänssler Verlag, 1979–88) for manuscripts and modern editions, and François Lesure, ed., *Recueils Imprimés XVIe–XVIIe Siècles*, series B/1 of *Répertoire International des Sources Musicales* (München-Duisburg: G. Henle, 1960) [RISM] for prints.

Manuscript Sources

BasU F.IX.22.	Basel. Öffentliche Bibliothek der Universität. MS F.IX.22
BerlPS 40098	Mus. ms 40098 from the collection of the former Preussische Staatsbibliothek, Berlin, preserved at present in the Biblioteka Jagiellónska, Krakow. ("Glogauer Liederbuch")
BerlSM 78.C.28	Berlin. Staatliche Museen der Stiftung Preussischer Kulturbesitz. Kupferstichkabinett. MS 78.C.28 (*olim* Hamilton 451)
BolC Q16	Bologna. Civico Museo Bibliografico Musicale. MS Q16 (*olim* 109)
BolC Q17	Bologna. Civico Museo Bibliografico Musicale. MS Q17 (*olim* 148)
Buxheim	Munich. Bayerische Staatsbibliothek, Handschriften-Inkunabelabteilung. MS Cim 352b ("Buxheimer Orgelbuch")
CopKB 1848	Copenhagen. Det Kongelige Bibliotek. MS Ny kongelige Samling 1848
DijM 517	Dijon. Bibliothèque Municipale. MS 517 (*olim* 295)
EscSL IV.a.24	El Escorial. Real Monasterio de San Lorenzo del Escorial, Biblioteca y Archivo de Música. MS IV.a.24
FlorBN BR 229	Florence. Biblioteca Nazionale Centrale. MS Banco Rari 229 (*olim* Magliabechi XIX. 59)
FlorBN Magl. 176	Florence. Biblioteca Nazionale Centrale. MS Magliabechi XIX. 176
FlorBN Magl. 178	Florence. Biblioteca Nazionale Centrale. MS Magliabechi XIX. 178
FlorR 2356	Florence. Biblioteca Riccardiana. MS 2356
HradKM 7	Hradec Králové. Krajske Muzeum, Knihovna (Regional Museum, Library). MS II A 7 ("Speciálník Codex")
JenaU 32	Jena. Universitätsbibliothek. MS 32
LucAS 238	Lucca. Archivio de Stato, Biblioteca Manoscritti. MS 238
MilD 2	Milan. Archivio della Veneranda Fabbrica del Duomo, Sezione Musicale. Librone 2 (*olim* 2268)
ModE M.1.11	Modena. Biblioteca Estense e Universitaria. MS α.M.1.11 (Lat. 454)
ModE M.1.12	Modena. Biblioteca Estense e Universitaria. MS α.M.1.12 (Lat. 455)
ModE M.1.13	Modena. Biblioteca Estense e Universitaria. MS α.M.1.13 (Lat. 456; *olim* V.H.10)
MonteA 871	Monte Cassino. Biblioteca dell'Abbazia. MS 871 (*olim* 871N)
MunBS Germ. 810	Munich. Bayerische Staatsbibliothek, Handschriften-Inkunabelabteilung. MS Germanicus monacensis 810 (*olim* Mus. 3232; Cim. 351a) ("Schedel Liederbuch")
MunBS Lat. 5023	Munich. Bayerische Staatsbibliothek, Handschriften-Inkunabelabteilung. MS Latinus monacensis 5023
NHavY 91	New Haven. Yale University, Beinecke Rare Book and Manuscript Library. MS 91 ("Mellon Chansonnier")
OpBP 714	Oporto. Biblioteca Pública Municipale. MS 714
ParisBN 57	Paris. Bibliothèque Nationale, Département de la Musique. MS Rés. Vmc. 57 ("Nivelle de la Chaussée Chansonnier")

ParisBNF 9346	Paris. Bibliothèque Nationale, Département des Manuscrits. Fonds français, MS 9346 ("Bayeux Manuscript")
ParisBNF 15123	Paris. Bibliothèque Nationale, Département des Manuscrits. Fonds français, MS 15123 (*olim* Suppl. 2637) ("Pixérécourt Chansonnier")
ParisBNN 4379	Paris. Bibliothèque Nationale, Département des Manuscrits. Nouvelles acquisitions françaises, MS 4379
ParisBNR 2973	Paris. Bibliothèque Nationale, Département des Manuscrits. Collection Rothschild, MS 2973 (shelf mark: 1.5.13) ("Cordiforme Chansonnier")
PavU 362	Pavia. Biblioteca Universitaria. MS Aldini 362 (*olim* 131.A.17)
PragP 47	Prague. Památník Národního Písemnictví, Strahovská Knihovna (Museum of Czech Literature, Strahov Library). MS D.G.IV.47
RomeC 2856	Rome. Biblioteca Casanatense. MS 2856 (*olim* O.V. 208)
SegC s.s.	Segovia. Archivo Capitular de la Catedral. MS s.s.
SevC 5-1-43	Seville. Catedral Metropolitana, Biblioteca Capitular y Colombina. MS 5-1-43 (*olim* Z Tab. 135. N.° 33)
SienBC K.I.2	Siena. Biblioteca Comunale degli Intronati. MS K.I.2
TrentC 89	Trent. Castello del Buonconsiglio, Monumenti e collezioni provinciali (ex Museo Provinciale d'Arte). MS 89
TrentC 90	Trent. Castello del Buonconsiglio, Monumenti e collezioni provinciali (ex Museo Provinciale d'Arte). MS 90
TrentC 91	Trent. Castello del Buonconsiglio, Monumenti e collezioni provinciali (ex Museo Provinciale d'Arte). MS 91
TrentM 93	Trent. Museo Diocesano. MS BL (commonly, but unofficially referred to as MS 93, in recognition of its relationship to TrentC 87–92)
VatG XIII.27	Vatican City. Biblioteca Apostolica Vaticana. MS Cappella Giulia XIII 27 ("Medici Codex")
VatS 35	Vatican City. Biblioteca Apostolica Vaticana. MS Cappella Sistina 35
VatS 51	Vatican City. Biblioteca Apostolica Vaticana. MS Cappella Sistina 51
VatSP B80	Vatican City. Biblioteca Apostolica Vaticana. MS San Pietro B 80
VatU 1411	Vatican City. Biblioteca Apostolica Vaticana. MS Urbinates Latini 1411
VerBC 755	Verona. Biblioteca Capitolare. MS DCCLV
VerBC 757	Verona. Biblioteca Capitolare. MS DCCLVII
VerBC 759	Verona. Biblioteca Capitolare. MS DCCLIX
VerBC 761	Verona. Biblioteca Capitolare. MS DCCLXI
WarU 2016	Warsaw. Biblioteka Uniwersytecka, Oddział Zbiorów Muzycznych. MS Mf. 2016 (*olim* Mus. 58)
WashLC L25	Washington, D.C. Library of Congress, Music Division. MS M2.1.L25 Case ("Laborde Chansonnier")
WashLC M6	Washington, D.C. Library of Congress, Music Division. MS M2.1.M6 Case ("Wolffheim Fragment")
WolfA 287	Wolfenbüttel. Herzog August Bibliothek. MS Guelferbytanus 287 extravagantium

Printed Sources

RISM 1501	Harmonice musices Odhecaton A. Venice: O. Petrucci, 1501.
RISM 1502[2]	Canti B numero cinquanta B. Venice: O. Petrucci, 1502.
RISM 1505[1]	Fragmenta missarum. Venice: O. Petrucci, 1505.
RISM 1513[4]	Quinquagena carminum. Mainz: P. Schöffer, 1513.
RISM [ca. 1535][14]	[Lieder zu 3 & 4 Stimmen]. [Frankfurt am Main: C. Egenolff] s.d.
RISM 1538[9]	Trium vocum carmina a diversis musicis composita. Nuremberg: H. Formschneider, 1538.

Reference Works and Modern Editions

AmbG	Ambros, August Wilhelm. *Geschichte der Musik*. 5 vols. Leipzig: F. E. C. Leuckart, 1887–1911.
AMMM	*Archivium Musices Metropolitanum Mediolanense*. Edited by Luciano Migliavacca et al. 16 vols. Milan: Veneranda Fabbrica del Duomo, 1958–69.
BarbirO	Barbireau, Jacques. *Opera omnia*. Edited by Bernard Meier. 2 vols. Corpus Mensurabilis Musicae, 7. American Institute of Musicology, 1954–57.
BrowFC	Brown, Howard Mayer, ed. *A Florentine Chansonnier from the Time of Lorenzo the Magnificent: Florence, Biblioteca Nazionale Centrale, MS Banco Rari 229*. 2 vols. Monuments of Renaissance Music, 7. Chicago: University of Chicago Press, 1983.
BurkJM	Burkholder, J. Peter. "Johannes Martini and the Imitation Mass of

	the Late Fifteenth Century." *Journal of the American Musicological Society* 38 (1985): 470–523.
DrozT	Droz, E., G. Thibault, and Y. Rokseth, eds. *Trois chansonniers français du XVe siècle*. Documents artistiques du XVe siècle, 4. Paris: n.p., 1927.
DTÖ	*Denkmäler der Tonkunst in Österreich*.
DufayO	Dufay, Guillaume. *Opera omnia*. 6 vols. Edited by Heinrich Besseler. Corpus Mensurabilis Musicae, 1. American Institute of Musicology, 1951–66.
EDM	*Das Erbe Deutscher Musik*.
EitWL	Eitner, Robert. "Das Walther'sche Liederbuch 1461 bis 1467." *Monatshefte für Musikgeschichte* 6 (1874): 147–60.
GomO	Gombosi, Otto. *Jacob Obrecht: Eine stilkritische Studie*. Leipzig: Breitkopf & Härtel, 1925.
GottliebC	Gottlieb, Louis. "The Cyclic Masses of Trent 89." Ph.D. diss., University of California, Berkeley, 1958.
HAM	Apel, Willi, and Archibald T. Davison, eds. *Historical Anthology of Music*. 2 vols. Cambridge: Harvard University Press, 1946.
HanenC	Hanen, Martha Knight, ed. *The Chansonnier El Escorial IV.a.24: Commentary and Edition*. 3 vols. Musicological Studies 36. Henryville, Ottawa, and Binningen: Institute of Medieval Music, 1983.
HewCB	Petrucci, Ottaviano. *Canti B Numero Cinquanta, Venice, 1502*. Edited by Helen Hewitt. Monuments of Renaissance Music, 2. Chicago: University of Chicago Press, 1967.
HewO	Petrucci, Ottaviano. *Harmonice Musices Odhecaton A*. Edited by Helen Hewitt and Isabel Pope. Cambridge: Mediaeval Academy of America, 1942.
JosephsE	Josephson, Nors. *Early Sixteenth-Century Sacred Music from the Papal Chapel*. 2 vols. American Institute of Musicology, 1982.
LederU	Lederer, Victor. *Über Heimat und Ursprung der mehrstimmigen Tonkunst*. Leipzig: C. F. W. Siegel, 1906.
LeverettP	Leverett, Adelyn Peck. "A Paleographical and Repertorial Study of the Manuscript Trento, Castello del Buonconsiglio, 91 (1378)." Ph.D. diss., Princeton University, 1990.
LlorCS	Llorens Cisteró, José Maria. *Capellae Sixtinae codices, musicis notis instructi sive manu scripti sive praelo excussi*. Vatican City: n.p., 1960.
MartiniS	Martini, Johannes. *Secular Pieces*. Edited by Edward G. Evans. Recent Researches in the Music of the Middle Ages and Early Renaissance, 1. Madison: A-R Editions, 1975.
MarxT	Marx, Hans Joachim, ed. *Tabulaturen des XVI. Jahrhunderts*. 2 vols. Basel: Bärenreiter, 1967–70.
MB	*Musica Britannica: A National Collection of Music*.
MorelM	Morelot, Louis Simon Stéphen Hughes. *De la musique au XVe siècle*. Paris: V. Didron, 1856.
NitschS	Nitschke, Wolfgang. *Studien zu den Cantus-firmus-Messen Guillaume Dufays*. 2 vols. Berliner Studien zur Musikwissenschaft, 13. Berlin: Merseburger, 1968.
ObrNE	Obrecht, Jacob. *Collected Works*. Edited by Barton Hudson. New Obrecht Edition. Utrecht: Vereniging voor Nederlandse Muziekgeschiedenis, 1983–97.
ObrW	Obrecht, Jacob. *Werken*. 30 vols. Edited by Johannes Wolf. Amsterdam and Leipzig, 1908–21; reprint, Farnborough, England: Gregg International Press, 1968.
OckW	Ockeghem, Johannes. *Collected Works*. 3 vols. Edited by Dragan Plamenac and Richard Wexler. American Institute of Musicology, 1947–92.
PerkMC	Perkins, Leeman L., and Howard Garey, eds. *The Mellon Chansonnier*. 2 vols. New Haven and London: Yale University Press, 1979.
RaphU	Raphael, Alfred. "Über einige Quodlibete mit dem Cantus firmus 'O rosa bella' und über dieses Lied selbst." *Monatshefte für Musikgeschichte* 31 (1899): 161–79.
ReynoldsPP	Reynolds, Christopher A. *Papal Patronage and the Music of St. Peters, 1380–1513*. Berkeley and Los Angeles: University of California Press, 1995.
SchavranMP	Schavran, Henrietta. "The Manuscript Pavia, Biblioteca Universitaria, Codice Aldini 362: A Study of Song Tradition in Italy circa

	1440–1480." 2 vols. Ph.D. diss., New York University, 1978.
StrohmMB	Strohm, Reinhard. *Music in Late Medieval Bruges*. Rev. ed. Oxford: Clarendon Press, 1990.
WolfH	Wolf, Johannes. *Handbuch der Notationskunde*. 2 vols. Leipzig, 1913–19; reprint, Hildesheim: Georg Olms, 1963.
WolfS	Wolf, Johannes, ed. *Sing- und Spielmusik aus älterer Zeit*. Leipzig: Quelle & Meyer, 1926.

Editorial Method

Each Mass has been transcribed from a single source. ModE M.1.13—a Ferrarese manuscript compiled in 1480–81 under Martini's supervision—was used as the primary source whenever possible, and concordant sources were used as necessary to correct scribal errors. The three Masses not in ModE M.1.13 are all found in unique sources, so there was no question regarding which manuscript to use as the primary source. Variants in the concordant sources are listed in the critical notes. Whenever a principal and concordant source have significantly different readings, both versions have been included, as in the Credo of *Missa Ma bouche rit*.

The following editorial rules have been applied in this edition:

1. The orthography of the original text has been adjusted to modern conventions without comment. Word division follows that of the *Liber Usualis*.

2. Rubrics providing significant performance information in the original are reproduced in the score. Other rubrics are reported in the critical notes.

3. The sources provide only a limited sketch of the text underlay, often only indicating the text to be used with no reference to the required underlay or how often it should be repeated. The editors display different styles of realizing the underlay, and performers should feel free to experiment in this regard. In the edition, text that appears in the source is set in roman typeface. In any voice, text that is added by the editor, and which does not appear in that voice in the source, is enclosed in square brackets. Textual repeats added by the editor, whether indicated in the manuscript or not, are enclosed in angle brackets. The text underlay is set so as to provide the minimum number of textual repetitions. In general, words are not broken across rests, and full repetitions of phrases are preferred to partial repetitions. The application of editorial text underlay attempts to avoid cadences in the middle of words and allows for the repetition of a common note on the same syllable in passages approaching a cadence. As an exception to this rule, however, when a voice enters after a rest for the final "chord" of a section, the last syllable of the prevailing word is added (e.g., the "-men" of "Amen" is supplied).

4. The original designation of voice parts is retained. If the part names are not noted in the source, they are generalized to Superius, Altus, Tenor, and Bassus. Part names are repeated in full at the beginning of each Mass movement but are abbreviated if the scoring changes within the movement. Abbreviations of part names are standardized to S, A, CT, T, and B.

5. The original clef, key signature, mensuration sign, and first notated pitch or ligature in each voice part, along with all initial rests, are shown in an incipit at the beginning of each Mass movement before the brace. The range of each voice is shown after the modern clef, key signature, and meter signature and shows the range of pitches as they appear in the modern clef. Voice parts are uniformly transcribed placing Superius parts in treble clef, Altus, Contratenor, and Tenor parts in transposed treble clef, and Bassus parts in bass clef.

6. All mensural signs of the same type are consistently transcribed in the same meter. Meter symbols are inserted in the score if they are of the same form as their modern equivalents. (Thus C and ¢ are retained and are not changed to $\frac{4}{4}$ or $\frac{2}{2}$.) Whenever the meter signature changes within a piece, the original mensuration sign is shown above each and every part which carries the metrical change, and a modern signature is added to the score if it is not already prevailing. Mensurations signs in the original which duplicate prevailing meters in the modern score are still shown above the staff where they occur. A modern time signature is supplied at the beginning of each movement. If the music of one or more parts changes from a duple to a triple meter or the reverse while at least one part remains in the opposite meter, groupette symbols are used to maintain a modern conception of meter.

7. The measures are numbered continuously through all parts of each Mass movement, and each Mass movement begins a new series of measure numbers. Barlines are added after every brevis. Barlines do not imply regular metrical stress. Thin-thick barlines are added at the close of complete Mass movements unless the movement concludes with a reprise of an earlier section. Double-barlines have been added at the close of internal sub-sections. Note values are consistently reduced by half in the ratio of 2:1, including passages in coloration.

8. The last note in the last measure of a Mass movement or one of its parts is transcribed as a brevis with fermata, regardless of its appearance in the

source, unless it arrives after a measure begins, in which case it is transcribed as a value sufficient to fill the measure, and it is also provided with a fermata. A final longa is transcribed as a brevis with a fermata. Notes that continue past a barline in the transcription are divided into appropriate values and connected with a tie, and the fermata appears over the last tied note. Fermatas that appear within musical passages are given only when in the original. Occasionally, a vocal part transmits several pitches simultaneously at a cadence; all pitches have been retained in the edition, as this may indicate that the part divides at this point to produce a fuller sonority.

9. Accidentals on the staff appear in the principal source and have their normal meanings in modern practice. Accidentals made superfluous by modern barring and convention are eliminated without comment. All ♯ or ♭ signs have been adjusted to the modern ♯, ♮, or ♭ according to context, without further comment. Accidentals conveying *musica ficta* are placed above the staff in small type. These accidentals are not to be understood as optional; the editors consider them obligatory in accordance with conventions of the time. These conventions include (a) raised leading tones, or lowered approach tones, at cadences; (b) accidentals that correct harmonic or melodic diminished or augmented fourths, fifths, or octaves; (c) accidentals that follow the principle of *una nota super la*, that is, those that prevent a melodic tritone when a voice ascends above *la* in the prevailing hexachord; (d) accidentals that achieve a progression to a perfect consonance from the nearest imperfect consonance; (e) a shift to the soft hexachord in all voices through the end of a phrase, when suggested by the contrapuntal context. Accidentals above the staff are valid only for the note over which they appear; they are repeated within a measure whenever necessary.

10. Ligatures and coloration in the original are shown by full and open horizontal brackets, respectively. Coloration that causes triplets is also shown either by placing the numeral "3" above the affected notes whether or not it appears in the original, or a change of meter. When unbeamed notes are involved (as in a triplet group consisting of a quarter note followed by an eighth), a horizontal bracket with the numeric label "3" encloses the notes of the groupette. *Signa congruentiae* appear in some sources, but as their significance seems to be limited to use as cues, they have been eliminated without comment.

Critical Notes

Citations here are by sigla, a full list of which appears at the front of the volume. The following additional abbreviations are used in the critical notes: A = altus, B = bassus, CT = contratenor, S = superius, T = tenor. Pitches are reported according to the system in which middle C = c'.

Each report includes:

Unique or primary source listed by sigla, location within the manuscript, and any attribution or headings given in the manuscript.

Concordant source(s) also listed by sigla, location within the manuscript, and any attribution or headings given in the manuscript.

References to books, editions, periodical articles, and dissertations in which information about the Mass may be found. (See "List of Sigla and Abbreviations.")

The critical notes list by Mass movement the significant variants including pitch, inflection, and rhythm found in the primary source, and this is followed by reports of differences found in the concordant sources. If variants from another source are included, the source is identified first, and a listing of the variants follows.

In the appendix to part 2, after each polyphonic model, the following information is given:

Primary source listed by sigla, location within the manuscript, and any attribution given in the manuscript.

Concordant source(s) also listed by sigla, location within the manuscript, and any attribution given in the manuscript.

References to books, editions, periodical articles, and dissertations in which information about the model may be found. (See "List of Sigla and Abbreviations.")

Changes to the primary source to document editorial emendations.

Text and Translation if needed.

Commentary if needed.

Missa Cela sans plus

Edited by Elaine Moohan.

Unique source. VatS 51, fols. 155v–165: headed "Jo Martini"; tenor incipit "Sela sans plus."

CREDO

M. 42, CT, ♭ before note 1; ○ before note 7.

AGNUS DEI

M. 24, note 1–m. 25, rest 1, T, longa.

Missa Coda di pavon

Edited by Elaine Moohan.

Primary source. ModE M.1.13, no. XI: headed "Io martini coda di pavon"; tenor incipit "Coda di pavon."

Concordant sources. MilD2, fols. 20v–26: headed "Io Mar," lacks Kyrie, "Confiteor," and Agnus Dei. SienBC K.1.2, fols. 131v–137, lacks "Confiteor," "Pleni," "Osanna," "Benedictus," and Agnus Dei. TrentC 91, fols. 167v–169: contrafacta of "Et in terra" and 12 measures of Agnus Dei 2 (not included here).

Reference. AMMM 12, pp. 9–28.

Kyrie

SienBC K.1.2. M. 10, S, notes 1–2, minim e′–minim f′. M. 12, S, note 2, d″. M. 14, note 1–m. 15, note 1, CT, brevis cum puncto additionis. M. 17, note 1–m. 18, note 1, T, brevis cum puncto additionis. M. 17, note 1–m. 18, note 1, B, brevis cum puncto additionis. M. 22, T, notes 1–3, brevis c′–minim b–minim a, colored notes. M. 26, note 1–m. 28, note 1, T, longa–longa. M. 29, S, notes 1–3, semibrevis e′–semibrevis e′. M. 29, T, rest 1, semibrevis c′. M. 30, T, notes 1–2, semibrevis b. M. 34, note 6–m. 35, note 2, S, semibrevis a′. M. 34, CT, notes 1–2, semibrevis cum puncto additionis. M. 37, B, note 2, ♭. M. 39, S, note 1, ♭. M. 41, S, notes 3–4, black semibrevis f″.

Gloria

MilD2. M. 3, CT, note 2, d′. M. 4, note 1–m. 5, note 1, CT, semibrevis–brevis. M. 17, B, note 1–rest 1, semibrevis g. M. 20, B, notes 1–2, semibrevis. M. 25, B, note 2, lacks ♭. M. 46, S, note 2, ♭. M. 57, S, note 2, semiminim b′–semiminim a′. M. 63, T, note 1, semibrevis–semibrevis. M. 73, B, note 2, lacks ♭. M. 79, B, note 1, lacks ♭. M. 80, S, notes 3–4, semibrevis cum puncto additionis b′–semiminim a′. M. 100, note 2–m. 101, note 1, S, brevis. M. 106, T, note 1, semibrevis–semibrevis. M. 117, B, note 1, lacks ♭. M. 124, CT, note 1, lacks ♭.

SienBC K.1.2. M. 2, B, notes 1–3, minim–minim–semibrevis. M. 3, B, note 1, minim–minim. M. 5, note 3–m. 6, note 2, S, semibrevis a′. M. 8, S, note 2, semiminim d′–semiminim c′. M. 8, note 2–m. 9, note 1, CT, brevis. M. 9, note 2–m. 10, note 1, CT, semibrevis–semibrevis. M. 9, T, note 2, c′. M. 17, B, note 1–rest 1, semibrevis g. M. 24, S, note 6, fusa e′–fusa f′. M. 35, S, notes 1–2, brevis. M. 35, CT, notes 1–2, brevis. M. 35, B, notes 1–2, brevis. M. 37, CT, notes 2–4, minim e′–semibrevis f′. M. 39, note 2–m. 40, note 1, CT, semibrevis cum puncto additionis. M. 40, B, notes 1–2, brevis–semibrevis. M. 42, S, notes 1–2, semibrevis. M. 43, note 2–m. 44, note 1, B, brevis. M. 45, CT, notes 3–4, semibrevis a′. M. 46, S, note 2, ♭. M. 48, CT, note 2, semiminim e′–semiminim d′. M. 53, T, note 1, semibrevis–semibrevis. M. 57, S, notes 2–4, semiminim b′–semiminim a′–semibrevis b′. M. 60, note 1–m. 61, note 1, CT, brevis–semibrevis. M. 66, S, note 1, semibrevis–semibrevis. M. 66, note 1–m. 67, note 1, B, brevis–semibrevis–semibrevis. M. 68, S, note 1, semibrevis–semibrevis. M. 68, note 1–m. 69, note 1, B, brevis–semibrevis–semibrevis. M. 72, CT, note 2, d′. M. 73, S, note 1, semibrevis–semibrevis. M. 73, T, note 1, semibrevis–semibrevis. M. 75, S, notes 1–2, brevis. M. 76, B, note 1, semibrevis–semibrevis. M. 80, S, notes 3–4, semibrevis b′–minim a′, in minor coloration. M. 88, S, notes 1–2, brevis. M. 91, S, note 2, semibrevis f′–minim e′, in minor coloration. M. 100, note 2–m. 101, note 1, S, brevis. M. 101, CT, note 2, semiminim f′–semiminim e′. M. 103, note 1–m. 104, note 1, T, brevis–semibrevis. M. 104, note 1–m. 105, note 1, S, minim c′–minim b′–semibrevis cum puncto additionis a′. M. 106, S, notes 2–4, semiminim f′–semiminim e′–semibrevis f′. M. 118, S, note 1, semibrevis–semibrevis. M. 118, CT, note 2, a. M. 119, B, note 1, semibrevis–semibrevis. M. 120, S, note 1, ♭. M. 123, T, note 1, semibrevis–semibrevis.

Credo

M. 133, note 2–m. 134, note 1, CT, g′.

MilD2. M. 1, T, notes 1–2, brevis. M. 1, B, notes 1–2, brevis. M. 2, T, notes 1–2, brevis. M. 20, CT, note 2, semibrevis–minim. M. 43, CT, note 2, lacks ♭. M. 43, B, note 2, lacks ♭. M. 67, CT, notes 2–3, semibrevis. M. 69, CT, note 1, minim–minim. M. 89, note 1–m. 90, note 1, T, brevis rest–brevis. M. 89, note 1–m. 90, note 2, B, semibrevis g–brevis g. M. 92, S, notes 1–3, brevis. M. 94, S, rest 1–note 1, brevis d″. M. 94, CT, note 1, minim–minim. M. 95, S, note 1, semibrevis rest. M. 100, CT, note 2, e′. M. 105, T, notes 1–2, minim cum puncto additionis f′–semiminim e′. M. 109, CT, note 3, lacks ♭. M. 109, B, note 3, lacks ♭. M. 111, S, longa c″. M. 111, CT, after note 4, longa g′. M. 111, T, longa c′. M. 111, B, longa c.

SienBC K.1.2. M. 2, S, note 2, minim–minim. M. 2, CT, note 1, semibrevis–semibrevis. M. 2, T, note 2, minim–minim. M. 2, B, note 2, minim–minim. M. 3, note 1–m. 4, note 1, S, minim–minim–semibrevis–minim. M. 3, T, note 1, semibrevis–semibrevis. M. 3, B, note 1, semibrevis–semibrevis. M. 4, note 3–m. 5, note 1, S, semibrevis–minim. M. 4, note 2–m. 5, note 1, CT, brevis–semibrevis. M. 4, B, note 1, lacks ♭. M. 6, note 2–m. 7, note 1, S, minim–minim–minim. M. 9, S, note 1, minim–minim. M. 10, S, note 2, g′. M. 12, CT, note 1, c′. M. 20, CT, note 2, semibrevis–minim. M. 36, note 5–m. 37, note 1, S, semibrevis a′–minim c″. M. 37, note 3–m. 38, note 2, S, semibrevis a′. M. 44, S, note 1, ♭. M. 45, S, rest 1–note 2, brevis f″. M. 51, T, note 2, semibrevis d′–minim c′, in minor coloration. M. 58, T, notes 3–4, minim cum puncto additionis c′–semiminim d′. M. 67, CT, notes 2–3, semibrevis. M. 69, B, notes 2–3, semibrevis. M. 71, CT, notes 1–2, semibrevis. M. 72, B, note 2, ♭. M. 74, B, note 1, semibrevis–minim. M. 85, B, note 2, ♭. M. 89, note 1–m. 90, note 1, T, brevis rest–brevis. M. 89, note 1–m. 90, note 1, B, semibrevis g–semibrevis g. M. 91, T, note 1, minim–minim–semibrevis. M. 92, S, notes 2–3, semibrevis.

M. 93, T, note 1, semibrevis–semibrevis.   M. 96, note 3–m. 97, note 2, S, semibrevis d".   M. 100, S, note 2, fusa c"–fusa b'   M. 100, note 6–m. 101, note 2, S, semibrevis a'.   M. 102, CT, notes 1–2, minim b–minim a.   M. 107, S, note 2, ♭.   M. 107, B, note 2, lacks ♭.   M. 110, note 4–m. 111, note 2, CT, semibrevis cum puncto additionis.   M. 111, S, longa c".   M. 111, CT, after note 4, longa g'.   M. 111, T, longa c'.   M. 111, B, longa c.

SANCTUS

MilD2. M. 6, T, note 3, ♭.   M. 8, S, note 4, lacks ♭.   M. 18, CT, note 3, lacks ♭.   M. 55, S, notes 6–8, minim cum puncto additionis a'–fusa g'–fusa f'.   M. 61, note 1–m. 62, note 1, CT, longa–semibrevis.   M. 63, CT, note 5, lacks ♭.   M. 63, B, note 3, lacks ♭.   M. 64, T, notes 3–4, semiminim–semiminim.   M. 74, B, note 2, lacks ♭.   M. 76, B, note 3, lacks ♭.   M. 89, B, note 4, lacks ♭.

SienBC K.1.2. M. 8, S, note 4, lacks ♭.   M. 14, B, note 4, lacks ♭.   M. 18, note 4–m. 19, note 2, S, semibrevis d".   M. 23, S, note 1, lacks ♭.

Missa In feuers hitz

Edited by Murray Steib.
Unique source. VerBC 759, fols. 15v–20: headed "Io. Martini."

AGNUS DEI

M. 5, B, note 6, minim c' added; a minim was left out at this point in the source, and c' makes the most contrapuntal sense.

Missa La Martinella

Edited by Murray Steib.
Unique source. VatS 35, fols. 38v–52: headed "Io. Martini."

KYRIE

M. 1, T, "Crescit in duplo."

GLORIA

M. 82, T, "Prima vice crescit in duplo, secunda vice ut jacet."   M. 190, T, "Crescit in duplo."

CREDO

M. 1, T, "Crescit in duplo."   M. 154, T, "Prima vice crescit in duplo, secunda ut jacet."   M. 235, T, "Prima vice crescit in duplo, secunda ut jacet."

SANCTUS

M. 108, T, "Prima vice crescit in duplo, secunda vice ut jacet." There is no rubric at the beginning of the movement, but the only possible solution is to read the semibrevis as perfect (containing three equal minims) and to augment the tenor by two the first time through.

Missa Ma bouche rit

Edited by Murray Steib.
Primary source. ModE M.1.13, no. VIII: headed "Io. Martini."
Concordant sources. VerBC 761, fols. 53v–62. MilD 2, fols. 26v–36 (lacking Kyrie and Agnus): headed "Io. Mar."
Reference. AMMM 12, pp. 32–56.

KYRIE

VerBC 761. M. 8, S, notes 2–3, minim cum puncto additionis e'–semiminim f'.   M. 15, note 3–m. 16, note 1, CT, longa d'.   M. 27, B, note 1, A.   M. 28, CT, note 1, minim e'–semiminim g'–semiminim f'.   M. 28, CT, note 6, fusa f'–fusa e'.   M. 28, B, notes 4–5, semibrevis b.   M. 29, CT, notes 3–4, semibrevis c'.   M. 35, S, notes 9–10, semiminim c'.   M. 36, CT, note 1, minim g'–semiminim g'.   M. 36, CT, notes 3–4, semiminim d'.

GLORIA

M. 19, S, note 3, e' changed to c' as in MilD 2 and VerBC 761, to avoid parallel fifths in the outer voices.

VerBC 761. M. 9, B, note 1, minim cum puncto additionis f–semiminim e.   M. 17, B, note 3, minim cum puncto additionis f–semiminim e.   M. 17, CT, note 6, minim cum puncto additionis b–semiminim a.   M. 22, S, note 3, semibrevis cum puncto additionis d"–minim c", in minor coloration.   M. 27, note 2–m. 28, note 1, S, minim rest semibrevis c"–minim a'.   M. 27, note 3–m. 29, note 1, CT, semiminim a'–semiminim g'–semiminim f'–semiminim e'–semibrevis f'–semibrevis g'–minim g'.   M. 30, CT, notes 2–3, semibrevis f'.   M. 32, CT, note 3, semibrevis a'–minim g' in minor coloration.   M. 47, CT, note 3, has B♭.   M. 48, S, note 2, minim cum puncto additionis b♭'–semiminim a'.   M. 50, note 2–m. 51, note 4, B, minim g–minim cum puncto additionis g–semiminim e–minim f–minim g–semiminim f–semiminim e.   M. 54, T, note 3, minim g.   M. 58, S, note 2, minim cum puncto additionis e'–semiminim d'.   M. 60, B, note 1, has B♭.   M. 62, CT, note 1, semibrevis e'–minim e'.   M. 73, S, note 2, semiminim a'–semiminim b'.   M. 74, CT, note 1, semibrevis e'–minim e'.   M. 107, S, note 2, semiminim g'–semiminim f'.   M. 119, rest 1–m. 121, note 1, CT, semibrevis c'–semibrevis rest–semiminim a–semiminim b–semiminim c'–semiminim d'–minim e'–semiminim f'–semiminim g'–minim a'.   M. 120, note 1–m. 121, note 1, S, semibrevis cum puncto additionis c"–minim c".   M. 125, note 1–m. 127, note 2, B, semibrevis e–semibrevis c (ligated)–minim rest–minim c–semibrevis e–minim d–semibrevis c–minim d.   M. 127, note 2–m. 128, note 1, CT, semibrevis g'–minim f'–minim e'.   M. 127, S, notes 2–4, semibrevis c"–semiminim b'–semiminim a'.   M. 127, T, notes 2–4, semibrevis e'–semiminim d'–semiminim c'.   M.

129, note 1–m. 130, note 1, CT, minim c'–semibrevis f'–minim e'–longa e'.

MilD 2. M. 9, B, note 1, minim cum puncto additionis f–semiminim e.   M. 17, CT, note 6, minim cum puncto additionis b–semiminim a.   M. 17, B, note 3, minim cum puncto additionis f–semiminim e.   M. 18, T, note 1, semibrevis rest.   M. 20, note 3–m. 21, note 1, CT, brevis c'.   M. 22, S, note 3, minim cum puncto additionis d"–semiminim c".   M. 24, note 3–m. 25, note 2, CT, semibrevis cum puncto additionis g'–semibrevis g'–minim g'.   M. 27, note 2–m. 28, note 1, S, minim rest–semibrevis c"–minim a'.   M. 30, T, notes 1–2, semibrevis cum puncto additionis c'.   M. 32, CT, note 3, minim cum puncto additionis a'–semiminim g'.   M. 36, note 2–m. 38, note 4, B, brevis c, semibrevis cum puncto additionis c, minim c, semibrevis g.   M. 48, S, note 2, minim cum puncto additionis b'–semiminim a'.   M. 58, S, note 2, minim cum puncto additionis e'–semiminim d'.   M. 62, CT, note 1, semibrevis e'–minim e'.   M. 73, S, note 2, semiminim a'–semiminim b'.   M. 119, note 1–m. 120, note 1, CT, semibrevis a'–minim a'.   M. 119, note 1–m. 120, note 1, B, brevis cum puncto additionis c'.   M. 120, note 2–m. 121, note 1, S, semibrevis cum puncto additionis c"–minim c".   M. 120, CT, note 2, semiminim g'–semiminim f'.   M. 120, note 4–m. 121, note 1, CT, minim cum puncto additionis a'–semiminim g'.   M. 125, note 1–m. 126, note 4, S, minim g'–minim rest–minim cum puncto additionis c'–semiminim d'–minim e'–minim f'.

Sanctus

M. 68, B, note 1, longa e; this measure is missing in ModE M.1.13, with the reading supplied from MilD 2 and VerBC 761.   M. 115, T, note 1, longa a; this measure is missing in ModE M.1.13, with the reading supplied from MilD 2 and VerBC 761.

VerBC 761. M. 5, CT, notes 2–3, semibrevis e'.   M. 17, note 2–m. 18, note 2, CT, semibrevis g'–semibrevis e'.   M. 20, note 1–m. 21, note 1, B, minim g–minim e–minim d–minim c–minim e–minim f.   M. 31, B, note 3, minim a–minim a.   M. 38, B, note 1, minim rest–minim e.   M. 39, S, notes 1–2, minim cum puncto additionis e'–semiminim f'.   M. 44, B, notes 3–5, minim cum puncto additionis f–semiminim e.   M. 52, S, note 2, minim a'–minim c".   M. 66, note 4–m. 67, note 2, S, minim cum puncto additionis a'–semiminim g'–minim f'–minim e'–semibrevis f'.   M. 69, CT, notes 1–5, colored notes; CT, notes 4–5, semibrevis f'; B, notes 1–4, colored notes.   M. 71, S, notes 1–3, semibrevis cum puncto additionis d"–semibrevis b', ligated.   M. 78, T, notes 1–4, colored notes.   M. 84, S and T, notes 1–4, colored notes.   M. 85, CT, notes 1–2, semibrevis cum puncto additionis b.   M. 86, CT, notes 1–4, colored notes.   M. 89, S, notes 2–3, semibrevis a'.   M. 96, note 3–m. 97, note 1, S, semibrevis g'–semibrevis g'.   M. 107, T, notes 2–3, minim c'–minim b.   M. 113, note 5–m. 114, note 2, S, minim f'–minim e'.   M. 115, B, note 1, longa A.

MilD 2. M. 3, CT, note 1, brevis e'–semibrevis e'.   M. 5, CT, notes 2–3, semibrevis e'.   M. 17, note 2–m. 18, note 1, CT, semibrevis g'–semibrevis e'.   M. 39, S, notes 1–2, minim cum puncto additionis e'–semiminim f'.   M. 44, S, note 1, minim b omitted.   M. 52, S, note 2, minim a'–minim c".   M. 69, B, notes 1–4, colored notes.   M. 71, S, notes 1–2, semibrevis cum puncto additionis d".   M. 72, CT, note 1, semibrevis a'.   M. 74, note 3–m. 75, note 2, T, colored notes.   M. 78, T, notes 1–4, colored notes.   M. 80, CT, note 2, semibrevis a' missing.   M. 84, T, notes 1–4, colored notes.   M. 87, CT, note 1, longa e'.   M. 96, note 3–m. 97, note 1, S, semibrevis g'–semibrevis g'.   M. 107, T, notes 2–3, minim c'–minim b.   M. 113, note 5–m. 114, note 2, S, minim f'–minim e'.   M. 115, B, note 1, longa A.

Agnus Dei

VerBC 761. M. 3, CT, note 2, minim a'.   M. 25, S, note 2, lacks b♭.   M. 37, B, notes 1–2, minim e–minim f.   M. 46, S, notes 2–3, minim cum puncto additionis a'–semiminim g'.   M. 71, note 5–m. 72, note 2, S, semibrevis f' (ligated with the following note).

Missa Or sus, or sus

Edited by Elaine Moohan.

Primary source. ModE M.1.13, no. I: sections of the Sanctus are copied Sanctus–Pleni sunt caeli/Osanna 1–Benedictus–Osanna 2; lacks Agnus Dei 2, which is provided from concordant sources.

Concordant sources. JenaU 32, fols. 220r–233r: sections of the Sanctus are copied Sanctus–Pleni sunt caeli–Benedictus–Osanna; lacks Agnus Dei 2. VatS 51, fols. 145v–155: headed "J Martini," tenor incipit "Orsus orsus"; lacks "Et incarnatus." VerBC 755, fols. 85v–95: tenor incipit "Orsus orsus par desus"; lacks "Et incarnatus." VerBC 761, fols. 89v–101: tenor incipit "Orsus orsus". LucAS 238, fols. 48v–48bisv: fragmentary source (not included here) containing Kyrie, S and T; "Et in terra," CT and B; "Qui tollis," S and T. The critical notes for each movement but the Kyrie are divided and labeled by section for easier reference.

Kyrie

The illuminated border has been cut away from the opening folio of ModE M.1.13, resulting in the loss of some notes of the superius and tenor on fol. 1v. These notes are supplied from concordant sources in the following places: M. 1, S; M. 1–6, T; M. 12, S, notes 1–2; M. 15, S; M. 15, T; M. 30 note 4–m. 31 note 1, S; M. 40, S; M. 40, T; M. 51 note 2–m. 52, note 2, S.

Emendation to the primary source: M. 44, CT, notes 3–4, minim d'.

JenaU 32. M. 11, T, note 3, minim g'–minim e'. M. 18, note 2–m. 19, note 1, S, semibrevis–minim. M. 20, note 2–m. 21, note 1, S, semibrevis cum puncto additionis g'–minim f'. M. 21, S, note 2, minim f'–mimim e'. M. 32, S, notes 1–3, minim cum puncto additionis c"–semiminim b'. M. 36, CT, notes 1–3, minim cum puncto additionis b–semiminim a. M. 41, CT, notes 1–4, under mensuration sign 3, semibrevis b–minim c'–minim d'–minim a–minim b. M. 42, CT, mensuration sign C. M. 43, T, note 4, semiminim d'–semiminim c'. M. 47, S, note 4, semiminim b'–semiminim c". M. 54, S, note 2, ♭. M. 54, note 4–m. 55, note 1, S, minim cum puncto additionis d"–semiminim c", in minor coloration.

VatS 51. M. 1, CT, notes 1–2, brevis rest. M. 1, B, rest 1, semibrevis cum puncto additionis c–minim d. M. 2, CT, notes 1–2, brevis c'. M. 2, B, notes 1–2, minim e–minim cum puncto additionis f–semiminim e–minim f. M. 4, B, notes 1–2, semibrevis–minim. M. 12, S, note 1, minim–minim. M. 12, note 3–m. 13, note 1, S, semibrevis d"–minim c", in minor coloration. M. 18, note 2–m. 19, note 1, S, semibrevis–minim. M. 20, note 2–m. 21, note 1, S, semibrevis cum puncto additionis g'–semiminim f'–semiminim e'. M. 30, note 4–m. 31, note 1, S, semibrevis d"–minim c", in minor coloration. M. 36, CT, note 4, ♯. M. 38, note 4, CT, minim f'–minim g'. M. 41, CT, notes 1–4, under mensuration sign 3, semibrevis b–minim c'–minim d'–minim a–minim b. M. 42, CT, mensuration sign C. M. 43, B, note 2, ♭. M. 45, CT, notes 3–4, minim cum puncto additionis c'–semiminim b–semiminim a. M. 46, B, note 2, lacks ♭. M. 49, S, notes 3–4, minim–minim. M. 50, S, note 2, minim cum puncto additionis a'–semiminim g'. M. 54, note 4–m. 55, note 1, S, minim cum puncto additionis d"–semiminim c". M. 56, CT, note 1, longa g'–longa e'.

VerBC 755. M. 1, CT, notes 1–2, brevis rest. M. 1, B, rest 1, semibrevis cum puncto additionis c–minim d. M. 2, CT, notes 1–2, brevis c'. M. 2, B, notes 1–2, minim e–minim cum puncto additionis f–semiminim e–minim f. M. 12, note 3–m. 13, note 1, S, semibrevis d"–minim c", in minor coloration. M. 15 to end, B, B♭ signature. M. 18, note 2–m. 19, note 1, S, semibrevis–minim. M. 20, note 2–m. 21, note 1, S, semibrevis cum puncto additionis g'–semiminim f'–semiminim e'. M. 30, note 4–m. 31, note 1, S, minim cum puncto additionis d"–semiminim c". M. 31, CT, note 3, lacking. M. 32, CT, note 1, d'. M. 36, CT, note 4, ♯. M. 38, CT, note 4, minim f'–minim g'. M. 41, CT, notes 1–4, under mensuration sign 3, semibrevis b–minim c'–minim d'–minim a–minim b. M. 42, CT, mensuration sign C. M. 43, B, note 2, ♭. M. 45, CT, notes 3–4, minim cum puncto additionis c'–semiminim b–semiminim b–semiminim a. M. 46, B, note 2, lacks ♭. M. 49, S, notes 3–4, minim–minim. M. 50, S, note 2, minim cum puncto additionis a'–semiminim g'. M. 54, S, note 2, ♭. M. 54, note 4–m. 55, note 1, S, minim cum puncto additionis d"–semiminim c". M. 56, CT, note 1, longa g'–longa e', ligated.

VerBC 761. M. 1, CT, notes 1–2, brevis rest. M. 1, B, rest 1, semibrevis cum puncto additionis c–minim d. M. 2, CT, notes 1–2, brevis c'. M. 2, B, notes 1–2, minim e–minim cum puncto additionis f–semiminim e–minim f. M. 4, B, notes 1–2, semibrevis–minim. M. 12, note 3–m. 13, note 1, S, semibrevis d"–minim c", in minor coloration. M. 13, CT, note 1, semibrevis–brevis. M. 20, note 2–m. 21, note 1, S, semibrevis cum puncto additionis g'–semiminim f'–semiminim e'. M. 29, S, notes 2–3, minim g'. M. 30, note 4–m. 31, note 1, S, semibrevis d"–minim c", in minor coloration. M. 38, CT, note 4, minim f'–minim g'. M. 41, CT, notes 1–4, under mensuration sign 3, semibrevis b–minim c'–minim d'–minim a–minim b. M. 42, CT, mensuration sign C. M. 43, B, note 2, ♭. M. 45, CT, notes 3–4, minim cum puncto additionis c'–semiminim b–semiminim b–semiminim a. M. 49, S, notes 3–4, minim–minim. M. 50, S, note 2, minim cum puncto additionis a'–semiminim g'. M. 54, note 4–m. 55 note 1, semibrevis d"–minim c", in minor coloration.

Gloria

Et in terra

JenaU 32. M. 9, note 1–m. 10, note 1, T, semibrevis–semibrevis cum puncto additionis. M. 15, note 1–m. 16, note 1, B, semibrevis–minim–minim–minim–minim. M. 16, CT, notes 1–2, minim–minim–minim–minim. M. 18, note 3–m. 19, note 1, S, minim cum puncto additionis d"–semiminim c". M. 20, B, notes 1–2, brevis. M. 21, B, note 1, lacks ♭. M. 23, T, note 1, semibrevis cum puncto additionis–minim. M. 24, T, notes 1–2, semibrevis. M. 26, S, note 5, minim cum puncto additionis a'–semiminim g'. M. 30, B, notes 1–2, semibrevis a–semibrevis c'–semibrevis c', colored notes. M. 34, CT, notes 1–2, minim d'. M. 46, CT, notes 1–2, brevis.

VatS 51. M. 9, note 2–m. 10, note 1, B, semibrevis–minim–minim. M. 11, note 1–m. 12, note 1, B, semibrevis–minim–minim–minim–minim. M. 13, note 4–m. 14, note 1, CT, semibrevis a'–minim g', in minor coloration. M. 15, note 2–m. 16, note 1, CT, minim–minim–minim–minim. M. 15, note 1–m. 16, note 1, B, minim cum puncto additionis–semiminim–minim–minim–minim–minim. M. 18, note 3–m. 19, note 1, S, semibrevis d"–minim c", in minor coloration. M. 26, note 5–m. 27, note 1, S, minim cum puncto additionis a'–semiminim g'. M. 41, B, note 1, minim–minim.   M. 47, note 1–m. 48, note 1, CT, semibrevis–semibrevis–longa.

VerBC 755. M. 3, B, notes 3–4, semibrevis e.   M. 8, B, note 1, ♭.   M. 9, note 2–m. 10, note 1, B, semibrevis–minim–minim.   M. 11, note 1–m. 12, note 1, B, semibrevis–minim–minim–minim–minim.   M. 13, note 4–m. 14, note 1, CT, semibrevis a'–minim g', in minor coloration.   M. 15, note 2–m. 16, note 1, CT, minim–minim–minim–minim.   M. 15, note 1–m. 16, note 1, B, minim cum puncto additionis–semiminim–minim–minim–minim–minim.   M. 18, note 3–m. 19, note 1, S, semibrevis d"–minim c", in minor coloration.   M. 26, note 5–m. 27, note 1, S, minim cum puncto additionis a'–semiminim g'.   M. 41, B, note 1, minim–minim.   M. 47, note 1–m. 48, note 1, CT, semibrevis–semibrevis–longa.

VerBC 761. M. 7, S, note 2, semibrevis e'''–minim d''', in minor coloration.   M. 9, note 1–m. 12, note 1, B, brevis–semibrevis–minim–minim–black semibrevis–black minim–minim–minim–minim–minim.   M. 13, note 4–m. 14, note 1, CT, semibrevis a'–minim g', in minor coloration.   M. 15, note 2–m. 16, note 1, CT, minim–minim–minim–minim.   M. 15, note 1–m. 16, note 1, B, minim cum puncto additionis–semiminim–minim–minim–minim–minim.   M. 18, note 3–m. 19, note 1, S, semibrevis d"–minim c", in minor coloration.   M. 21, B, note 1, lacks ♭.   M. 26, note 5–m. 27, note 1, S, semibrevis a'–minim g', in minor coloration.   M. 30, B, notes 1–2, semibrevis–semibrevis, ligated.   M. 39, note 3–m. 40, note 2, B, semibrevis f.   M. 41, B, note 1, minim–minim.   M. 47, note 1–m. 48, note 1, CT, semibrevis–semibrevis–longa.

Qui tollis

JenaU 32. M. 55, CT, notes 1–2, minim cum puncto additionis e'–fusa d'–fusa c'.   M. 57, note 3–m. 58, note 1, CT, minim cum puncto additionis d'–semiminim c'.   M. 63, CT, note 1, semibrevis–minim.   M. 69, note 2–m. 70, note 1, CT, semibrevis–minim.   M. 69, B, note 1, ♭.   M. 73, note 1–m. 74, note 1, T, brevis cum puncto additionis.   M. 74, note 1–m. 76, note 1, CT, brevis cum puncto additionis–semibrevis–brevis. M. 74, note 1–m. 75, note 1, B, brevis cum puncto additionis–semibrevis.   M. 76, T, note 1, semibrevis–semibrevis.   M. 77, note 1–m. 78, note 3, CT, minim cum puncto additionis–semiminim–minim–minim–semibrevis.   M. 77, note 1–m. 78, note 1, B, semibrevis cum puncto additionis–minim–minim–minim–semibrevis.   M. 86, note 1–m. 87, note 1, CT, brevis–brevis.   M. 92, note 3–m. 93, note 3, S, brevis. M. 111, note 4–m. 112, note 1, S, minim cum puncto additionis d"–semiminim c".   M. 122, CT, note 2, a. M. 136, B, notes 1–2, brevis cum puncto additionis. M. 140, CT, notes 1–2, perfect brevis b.   M. 140, T, perfect brevis.

VatS 51. M. 49, note 1–m. 50, note 1, CT, brevis–semibrevis–semibrevis.   M. 51, note 2–m. 52, note 2, CT, semibrevis cum puncto additionis c'–minim b–minim b–minim a.   M. 55, CT, note 2, semiminim d'–semiminim c'.   M. 57, note 2–m. 58, note 1, CT, minim cum puncto additionis e'–semiminim d'–minim cum puncto additionis d'–semiminim c'.   M. 61, note 1–m. 66, note 1, B, maxima– longa.   M. 64, S, notes 1–2, minim cum puncto additionis–semiminim.   M. 66, CT, note 1, semibrevis– minim.   M. 67, CT, notes 2–3, minim c'. M. 69, B, note 1, ♭.   M. 74, note 1–m. 76, note 1, CT, brevis– semibrevis–semibrevis–brevis.   M. 74, note 1–m. 78, note 1, B, brevis–semibrevis–semibrevis– semibrevis–semibrevis–semibrevis–brevis. M. 77, note 3–m. 78, note 1, S, semibrevis e"–minim d", in minor coloration.   M. 94, note 1–m. 95, note 1, B, semibrevis rest–semibrevis g–minim e.   M. 105, B, note 1, semibrevis rest–semibrevis d'. M. 107, note 4–m. 108, note 1, CT, semibrevis a'–minim g', in minor coloration.   M. 110, note 4–m. 111, note 2, S, semibrevis c"–semibrevis f".   M. 111, note 4–m. 112, note 1, S, semibrevis d"–minim c", in minor coloration. M. 111, note 4–m. 112, note 1, CT, semibrevis–minim. M. 111, B, note 1, ♭.   M. 118, S, notes 1–2, semibrevis cum puncto additionis g'–minim f'–minim cum puncto additionis f'–semiminim e'.   M. 126, S, notes 1–2, semibrevis cum puncto additionis c"–minim b'–minim b'–minim a'.   M. 128, CT, notes 1–3, semibrevis f'–brevis b'.   M. 128, B, note 1, semibrevis cum puncto additionis–minim.   M. 140, T, notes 1–2, perfect brevis.   M. 141, CT, note 1–2, perfect brevis.   M. 144, note 1–m. 145, note 1, CT, longa.

VerBC 755. M. 49, note 1–m. 50, note 1, CT, brevis–semibrevis–semibrevis.   M. 51, note 2–m. 52, note 2, CT, semibrevis cum puncto additionis c'–minim b–minim b–minim a.   M. 55, CT, note 2, semiminim d'–semiminim c'.   M. 57, note 3–m. 58, note 1, CT, minim cum puncto additionis d'–semiminim c'.   M. 61, note 1–m. 66, note 1, B, maxima. M. 64, S, notes 1–2, minim cum puncto additionis–semiminim.   M. 66, CT, note 1, semibrevis–minim. M. 69, B, note 1, ♭.   M. 74, note 1–m. 76, note 1, CT, brevis–semibrevis–semibrevis–brevis.   M. 74, note 1–m. 78, note 1, B, brevis–semibrevis–semibrevis–semibrevis–semibrevis–semibrevis–semibrevis–brevis. M. 77 note 3–m. 78, note 1, S, semibrevis e"–minim d", in minor coloration.   M. 105, B, note 1, semibrevis rest–semibrevis d'.   M. 107, note 4–m. 108, note 1, CT, semibrevis a'–minim g', in minor coloration.   M. 111, note 4–m. 112, note 1, S, semibrevis d"–minim c", in minor coloration.   M. 111, note 4–m. 112, note 1, CT, minim–minim–minim.   M. 111, B, note 1, ♭. M. 118, S, notes 1–2, semibrevis cum puncto additionis g'–minim f'–minim cum puncto additionis f'–semiminim e'. M. 126, S, notes 1–2, semibrevis cum puncto additionis c"–minim b'–minim b'–minim a'. M. 128, CT, note 3, ♭. M. 128, B, note 1, semibrevis cum puncto additionis–minim. M. 140, T, notes 1–2, perfect brevis. M. 141, CT, notes 1–2, perfect brevis. M. 143, B, note 3, ♭. M. 144, note 1–m. 145, note 1, CT, longa.

VerBC 761. M. 49, note 1–m. 50, note 1, CT, brevis–semibrevis–semibrevis. M. 51, note 2–m. 52, note 2, CT, semibrevis cum puncto additionis c'–minim b–minim cum puncto additionis b–semiminim a. M. 55, CT, note 2, semiminim d'–semiminim c'. M. 57, note 2–m. 58, note 1, minim cum puncto additionis e'–semiminim d'–minim cum puncto additionis d'–semiminim c'. M. 61, note 1–m. 66, note 1, T, maxima. M. 61, note 1–m. 66, note 1, B, maxima–longa. M. 64, S, notes 1–2, minim cum puncto additionis–semiminim. M. 67, CT, notes 2–3, minim c'. M. 69, B, note 1, ♭. M. 74, note 1–m. 76, note 1, CT, brevis–semibrevis–semibrevis–brevis. M. 74, note 1–m. 78, note 1, B, brevis–semibrevis–semibrevis–semibrevis–semibrevis–semibrevis–brevis. M. 77, note 3–m. 78, note 1, S, semibrevis e"–minim d", in minor coloration. M. 84, S, note 2, ♭. M. 94, note 1–m. 95, note 1, B, semibrevis rest–semibrevis g–minim e. M. 105, note 1–m. 106, note 1, B, semibrevis rest–semibrevis cum puncto additionis d'. M. 107, note 4–m. 108, note 1, CT, semibrevis a'–minim g', in minor coloration. M. 110, note 4–m. 111, note 2, S, semibrevis c"–semibrevis f". M. 111, note 4–m. 112, note 1, S, semibrevis d"–minim c", in minor coloration. M. 111, note 4–m. 112, note 1, CT, semibrevis–minim. M. 111, B, note 1, ♭. M. 118, S, notes 1–2, semibrevis cum puncto additionis g'–minim f'–minim f'–minim e'. M. 122, CT, note 3, minim b–minim a. M. 126, S, notes 1–2, semibrevis cum puncto additionis c"–minim b'–minim b'–minim a'. M. 128, B, note 1, semibrevis cum puncto additionis–minim. M. 140, T, notes 1–2, perfect brevis. M. 141, CT, notes 1–2, perfect brevis. M. 144, S, semibrevis cum puncto additionis c"–minim b'–minim b'–minim a'. M. 144, note 1–m. 145, note 1, CT, brevis–semibrevis–longa.

Credo

M. 119, B, note 1, a.

Patrem

JenaU 32. M. 5, B, note 1, semibrevis–semibrevis. M. 9, note 1–m. 10, note 1, T, longa–brevis. M. 9, note 1–m. 10, note 1, B, brevis–brevis. M. 11, S, notes 1–2, semibrevis cum puncto additionis a'–minim a'. M. 11, CT, note 1, f'. M. 11, B, notes 1–2, brevis f. M. 12, CT, note 1, minim–minim. M. 15, B, notes 1–2, semibrevis cum puncto additionis–minim. M. 16, B, notes 1–2, semibrevis–minim. M. 18, S, notes 2–3, semibrevis. M. 18, B, note 1, semibrevis cum puncto additionis–minim. M. 19, note 3–m. 21, note 1, T, brevis–brevis. M. 19, note 2–m. 20, note 1, B, semibrevis–minim–minim. M. 20, S, note 1, minim–minim. M. 21, B, note 2, lacks ♭. M. 23, note 1–m. 24, note 1, CT, brevis cum puncto additionis–minim rest. M. 23, T, notes 1–2, semibrevis cum puncto additionis–minim. M. 23, B, note 1, semibrevis–semibrevis. M. 30, CT, note 2, minim cum puncto additionis a'–semiminim g'. M. 32, S, notes 1–2, semibrevis. M. 39, note 4–m. 40, note 1, S, minim e'–minim d". M. 40, note 3–m. 42, note 2, B, minim–minim–semibrevis–minim–minim–minim–minim–minim–minim. M. 44, T, notes 1–2, semibrevis cum puncto additionis. M. 44, B, notes 1–5, semibrevis g–minim cum puncto additionis g–semiminim f. M. 45, S, notes 1–2, minim–minim. M. 45, note 4–m. 46, note 1, S, minim cum puncto additionis a'–semiminim g'. M. 45, T, note 1, minim–minim. M. 45, B, notes 1–3, minim e–minim d–minim c–minim f. M. 46, CT, note 2, c'. M. 47, CT, note 3, a. M. 47, note 1–m. 49, note 2, B, semibrevis cum puncto additionis–semibrevis cum puncto additionis–semibrevis–semibrevis–minim–minim. M. 48, S, note 2, minim–minim. M. 48, CT, notes 2–3, semibrevis. M. 48, note 1–m. 49, note 3, T, semibrevis–minim–minim–minim–minim. M. 49, CT, note 3, minim–minim. M. 50, CT, note 1, minim–minim. M. 51, B, notes 2–3, semibrevis f.

VatS 51. The "Patrem" starts one semibrevis later than in the primary source. It lacks the three-voice "Et incarnatus." M. 1, note 2–m. 2, note 2, S, semibrevis c"–minim c"–minim b' (omits m. 1, note 1). Mm. 1–8, T, 7 brevis rests + 1 semibrevis rest. M. 1, note 2–m.2, note 2, B, semibrevis cum puncto additionis c–minim d (omits m. 1, note 1). M. 2, note 2–m. 3, note 3, CT, semibrevis c'–minim c'–minim c'–minim b–minim b (omits m. 2, note 1). M. 3, B, notes 4–5, semibrevis g. M. 15, note 2–m. 16, note 2, CT, minim–minim–semibrevis. M. 18, B, note 1, semibrevis–minim–minim. M. 19, CT, notes 2–3, semibrevis d'. M. 19, note 2–m. 20, note 2, B, semibrevis–semibrevis–minim–minim. M. 23, S, notes 3–4, minim cum puncto additionis—semiminim. M. 23, T, note 2, minim–minim. M. 24, CT, note 1, semibrevis–minim rest. M. 28, S, note 3, a'. M. 30, CT, note 2, semibrevis a'–minim g', in minor coloration. M. 39, note 4–m. 40, note 1, S, minim e"–semiminim d"–semiminim c". M. 40, note 3–m. 41, note 1, B, minim–minim–semibrevis–minim–minim. M. 42, note 2–m. 43, note 1, B, minim–minim–minim–minim. M. 44, B, notes 3–5, minim e–semibrevis d, in minor coloration. M. 45, note 4–m. 46, note 1, S, minim cum puncto additionis a'–semiminim g'. M. 45, B, note 1, minim cum puncto additionis c–semiminim d. M. 47, B, note 1, semibrevis–minim, in minor coloration. M. 47, note

3–m. 48, note 1, B, semibrevis–minim, in minor coloration. M. 48, note 3–m. 50, note 1, B, minim–minim cum puncto additionis–semiminim–minim–minim–minim–minim–minim. M. 49, note 2–m. 50, note 1, CT, semibrevis–minim–minim–minim. M. 53, T, note 2, minim cum puncto additionis d′–semiminim c′. M. 54, note 3–m. 55, note 1, S, semibrevis d″–minim c″, in minor coloration. M. 54, T, note 4, b.

VerBC 755. The "Patrem" starts one semibrevis later than in the primary source. It lacks the three-part "Et incarnatus." M. 1, note 2–m. 2, note 2, S, semibrevis c″–minim c″–minim b′ (omits m. 1, note 1). Mm. 1–8, T, 7 brevis rests + 1 semibrevis rest. M. 1, note 2–m.2, note 2, B, semibrevis cum puncto additionis c–minim d (omits m. 1, note 1). M. 2, note 2–m. 3, note 3, CT, semibrevis c′–minim c′–minim c′–minim b–minim b (omits m. 2, note 1). M. 3, B, notes 4–5, semibrevis g. M. 15, note 2–m. 16, note 2, CT, minim–minim–semibrevis. M. 18, B, note 1, semibrevis–minim–minim. M. 19, CT, notes 1–2, semibrevis b–minim c′. M. 19, note 2–m. 20, note 2, B, semibrevis–semibrevis–minim–minim. M. 23, S, notes 3–4, minim cum puncto additionis–semiminim. M. 23, T, note 2, minim–minim. M. 24, CT, note 1, semibrevis–minim rest. M. 30, CT, note 2, minim cum puncto additionis a′–semiminim g′. M. 39, note 4–m. 40, note 1, S, minim e″–semiminim d″–semiminim c″. M. 40, note 3–m. 41, note 1, B, minim–minim–semibrevis–minim–minim. M. 42, note 2–m. 43, note 1, B, minim–minim–minim–minim. M. 44, B, notes 3–5, minim e–semibrevis d, in minor coloration. M. 45, note 4–m. 46, note 1, S, minim cum puncto additionis a′–semiminim g′. M. 45, B, note 1, minim cum puncto additionis c–semiminim d. M. 47, B, note 1, semibrevis–minim, in minor coloration. M. 47, note 3–m. 48, note 1, B, semibrevis–minim, in minor coloration. M. 48, note 3–m. 50, note 1, B, minim–minim cum puncto additionis–semiminim–minim–minim–minim–minim–minim. M. 49, note 2–m. 50, note 1, CT, semibrevis–minim–minim–minim. M. 53, T, note 2, minim cum puncto additionis d′–semiminim c′. M. 54, note 3–m. 55, note 1, S, semibrevis d″–minim c″, in minor coloration. M. 54, T, note 4, b.

VerBC 761. The "Patrem" starts one semibrevis later than in the primary source. M. 1, note 2–m. 2, note 2, S, semibrevis c″–minim c″–minim b′ (omits m. 1, note 1). Mm. 1–8, T, 7 brevis rests + 1 semibrevis rest. M. 1, note 2–m.2, note 2, B, semibrevis cum puncto additionis c–minim d (omits m. 1, note 1). M. 2, note 2–m. 3, note 3, CT, semibrevis c′–minim c′–minim c′–minim b–minim b (omits m. 2, note 1). M. 3, B, notes 4–5, semibrevis g. M. 15, note 2–m. 16, note 2, CT, minim–minim–semibrevis. M. 18, B, note 1, semibrevis–minim–minim. M. 19, note 2–m. 20, note 2, B, semibrevis–semibrevis–minim–minim. M. 23, S, notes 3–4, minim cum puncto additionis–semiminim. M. 23, T, note 2, minim–minim. M. 24, CT, note 1, semibrevis–minim rest. M. 30, CT, note 2, semibrevis a′–minim g′, in minor coloration. M. 39, note 4–m. 40, note 1, S, minim e″–semiminim d″–semiminim c″. M. 40, note 3–m. 41, note 1, B, minim–minim–semibrevis–minim–minim. M. 42, note 2–m. 43, note 1, B, minim–minim–minim–minim. M. 44, B, notes 3–5, minim e–semibrevis d, colored notes. M. 45, note 4–m. 46, note 1, S, semibrevis a′–minim g′, in minor coloration. M. 45, B, note 1, minim cum puncto additionis c–semiminim d. M. 47, B, note 1, semibrevis–minim, in minor coloration. M. 47, note 3–m. 48, note 1, B, semibrevis–minim, in minor coloration. M. 48, note 3–m. 51, note 1, B, minim–black semibrevis–black minim–minim–minim–minim–minim–minim–semibrevis cum puncto additionis. M. 49, note 2–m. 50, note 1, CT, semibrevis–minim–minim–minim. M. 53, T, note 2, semibrevis d′–minim c′, in minor coloration. M. 54, note 3–m. 55, note 1, semibrevis d″–minim c″, in minor coloration. M. 54, T, note 4, b. M. 55, note 1–m. 56, note 1, CT, longa.

Et incarnatus

JenaU 32. M. 57, note 1–m. 58, note 2, S, brevis cum puncto additionis c″–semibrevis c″. M. 62, S, notes 2–4, semiminim f′–semiminim e′–semibrevis f′. M. 68, note 5–m. 69, note 1, CT, minim cum puncto additionis d′–semiminim c′. M. 71, CT, note 1, minim cum puncto additionis f′–fusa e′–fusa f′. M. 74, S, note 2, semiminim b′–semiminim a′. M. 82, CT, note 4, minim cum puncto additionis b–semiminim a. M. 85, note 3–m. 86, note 2, CT, minim g′–minim cum puncto additionis e′–semiminim d′–semibrevis c′. M. 85, note 2–m. 86, note 3, B, black semibrevis g–black minim f–semibrevis e. M. 89, B, rest 1, minim g.

VerBC 761. M. 68, note 5–m. 69, note 1, CT, semibrevis d′–minim c′, in minor coloration. M. 71, note 4–m. 72, note 1, S, semibrevis d″–minim c″, in minor coloration. M. 90, note 4–m. 91, note 1, S, semibrevis e″–minim c″, in minor coloration.

Crucifixus

JenaU 32. M. 97, S, notes 1–2, brevis. M. 97, T, notes 1–2, brevis. M. 98, note 1–m. 99, note 1, T, brevis cum puncto additionis–semibrevis. M. 102, CT, note 2, lacks ♭. M. 107, B, note 1, semibrevis–semibrevis. M. 108, B, notes 1–2, brevis. M. 110, note 1–m. 113, note 1, B, semibrevis–semibrevis–semibrevis cum puncto additionis–minim–semibrevis–semibrevis–semibrevis–semibrevis rest. M. 116, note 2–m. 117, note 1, S, brevis. M. 116, note 1–m. 117, note 2, T, brevis–semibrevis. M. 116, note 1–m. 117, note 2, B, brevis–semibrevis. M. 126, T, note 1, semibrevis–semibrevis. M. 134, note 1–m. 135, note 1, T, brevis–semibrevis. M. 140, note 1–m. 141, note 1, T, brevis–brevis. M. 143, note 1–m. 144, note 1, T, brevis–brevis. M. 143, B, note 1, semibrevis–minim. M. 145, note 1–m. 146, note 1, T, brevis cum puncto additionis–semibrevis.

M. 171, T, note 1, brevis–semibrevis rest. M. 171, B, note 1, imperfect brevis–semibrevis rest. M. 172, T, rest 1–note 1, imperfect brevis c'–semibrevis c'. M. 172, B, note 1, imperfect brevis–semibrevis. M. 175, S, note 2, semibrevis cum puncto additionis a'–minim g'. M. 175, B, note 3, d. M. 183, S, notes 1–2, semibrevis cum puncto additionis c"–semiminim b'–semiminim a'–semibrevis b'. M. 185, CT, notes 2–3, semibrevis cum puncto additionis. M. 187, T, note 1, semibrevis cum puncto additionis–minim–semibrevis. M. 188, S, notes 2–3, minim a'–semibrevis a'. M. 193, CT, notes 1–4, imperfect brevis c'–semibrevis b. M. 195, S, note 1, semibrevis–semibrevis. M. 201, CT, note 3, f'. M. 203, S, note 1, semibrevis–semibrevis. M. 204, T, note 1, imperfect brevis–semibrevis. M. 212, CT, notes 1–2, semibrevis–semibrevis. M. 214, S, note 3, minim a'–minim b'. M. 214, T, notes 1–2, perfect brevis. M. 219, S, notes 1–3, imperfect brevis g'. M. 224, S, notes 1–3, imperfect brevis c".

VatS 51. M. 102, CT, note 1, lacks ♭. M. 111, note 1–m. 113, note 1, B, semibrevis–semibrevis–semibrevis–semibrevis–semibrevis–semibrevis rest. M. 121, CT, note 2, g'. M. 126, CT, note 2, semiminim f'–semiminim e'. M. 140, note 2–m. 141, note 1, B, semibrevis cum puncto additionis. M. 171, T, note 1, imperfect brevis–semibrevis rest. M. 172, T, rests 1–2 and note 1, perfect brevis c'. M. 175, S, note 2, semibrevis cum puncto additionis a'–minim g'. M. 183, S, notes 1–2, semibrevis cum puncto additionis c"–minim b'–minim cum puncto additionis b'–semiminim a'. M. 185, CT, notes 2–3, semibrevis cum puncto additionis. M. 187, T, note 1, brevis–semibrevis. M. 204, note 1–m. 205, note 2, T, brevis–semibrevis–perfect brevis. M. 205, B, note 1–rest 1, perfect brevis. M. 214, T, notes 1–2, perfect brevis. M. 223, S, notes 2–3, brevis d". M. 223, B, note 3, ♭. M. 224, S, notes 2–4, minim b'–minim cum puncto additionis b'–semiminim a'.

VerBC 755. M. 111, note 1–m. 113, note 1, B, semibrevis–semibrevis–semibrevis–semibrevis–semibrevis–semibrevis rest. M. 126, CT, note 2, semiminim f'–semiminim e'. M. 171, T, note 1, imperfect brevis–semibrevis rest. M. 172, T, rests 1–2 and note 1, perfect brevis c'. M. 175, S, note 2, semibrevis cum puncto additionis a'–minim g'. M. 183, S, notes 1–2, semibrevis cum puncto additionis c"–minim b'–minim cum puncto additionis b'–semiminim a'. M. 185, CT, notes 2–3, semibrevis cum puncto additionis. M. 187, T, note 1, brevis–semibrevis. M. 204, note 1–m. 205, note 2, T, brevis–semibrevis–perfect brevis. M. 205, B, note 1–rest 1, perfect brevis. M. 214, T, notes 1–2, perfect brevis. M. 223, S, notes 2–3, brevis d". M. 223, B, note 3, ♭. M. 224, S, notes 2–4, minim b'–minim cum puncto additionis b'–semiminim a'.

VerBC 761. M. 102, CT, note 1, lacks ♭. M. 111, note 1–m. 113, note 1, B, semibrevis–semibrevis–semibrevis–semibrevis–semibrevis–semibrevis rest. M. 114, T, note 1, lacking. M. 121, S, note 1, minim–minim–minim. M. 121, CT, note 2, g'. M. 126, CT, note 2, semiminim f'–semiminim e'. M. 139, B, notes 1–2, semibrevis cum puncto additionis f. M. 140, note 1–m. 142, note 1, T, longa cum puncto additionis. M. 140, B, note 2, minim rest–minim c. M. 171, T, note 1, imperfect brevis–semibrevis rest. M. 172, T, rests 1–2 and note 1, perfect brevis c'. M. 175, S, note 2, semibrevis cum puncto additionis a'–minim g'. M. 183, S, notes 1–2, semibrevis cum puncto additionis c"–minim b'–minim b'–minim a'. M. 185, CT, notes 2–3, semibrevis cum puncto additionis. M. 187, T, note 1, brevis–semibrevis. M. 204, note 1–m. 206, note 1, T, brevis–semibrevis–imperfect longa. M. 205, B, note 1–rest 1, perfect brevis. M. 219, S, notes 1–3, brevis g'. M. 223, S, notes 2–3, brevis d". M. 224, S, notes 2–4, minim b'–minim b'–minim a'. M. 224, CT, note 1, brevis–semibrevis.

Sanctus

Sanctus

JenaU 32. M. 4, S, note 3, minim cum puncto additionis a'–semiminim g'. M. 11, CT, notes 1–3, minim cum puncto additionis g'–fusa f'–fusa e'. M. 11, B, note 1–rest 1, minim cum puncto additionis d'–semiminim c'–semiminim b–semiminim a.

Vat S 51. M. 4, S, note 3, minim cum puncto additionis a'–semiminim g'. M. 6, B, notes 3–5, semibrevis g–semiminim f–semiminim e. M. 8, B, note 1, ♭. M. 10, B, note 3, minim cum puncto additionis c'–semiminim b. M. 15, note 4–m. 16, note 1, T, minim cum puncto additionis d'–semiminim c'. M. 15, B, notes 1–2, minim cum puncto additionis–semiminim. M. 21, S, note 6, minim cum puncto additionis f'–semiminim e'. M. 21, CT, notes 1–4, minim f'–minim c'–minim cum puncto additionis d'–semiminim c'. M. 26, note 1–m. 27, note 1, T, brevis–semibrevis. M. 26, B, rest 1, minim c.

VerBC 755. M. 4, S, note 3, minim cum puncto additionis a'–semiminim g'. M. 6, B, notes 3–5, semibrevis g–semiminim f–semiminim e. M. 8, B, note 1, ♭. M. 10, B, note 3, minim cum puncto additionis c'–semiminim b. M. 15, note 4–m. 16, note 1, T, minim cum puncto additionis d'–semiminim c'. M. 21, S, note 6, minim cum puncto additionis f'–semiminim e'. M. 26, note 1–m. 27, note 1, T, brevis–semibrevis. M. 26, B, rest 1, minim c.

VerBC 761. M. 4, S, note 3, minim cum puncto additionis a'–semiminim g'. M. 6, B, notes 3–5, semibrevis g–semiminim f–semiminim e. M. 8, B, note 1, ♭. M. 10, B, note 3, semibrevis c'–minim b, in minor coloration. M. 15, note 4–m. 16, note 1, T, semibrevis d'–minim c', in minor coloration. M. 15, B, notes 1–2, minim cum puncto additionis–semiminim. M. 21, S, note 6, minim cum puncto additionis f'–semiminim e'. M. 21, CT, notes 1–4, minim f'–minim c'–minim cum puncto additionis d'–semiminim c'. M. 26, note 1–m. 27, note 1, T, brevis–semibrevis. M. 26, B, rest 1, minim c.

Pleni sunt caeli

JenaU 32. M. 36, note 5–m. 37, note 1, CT, minim cum puncto additionis c′–semiminim d′. M. 37, CT, note 2, semiminim b–semiminim a. M. 42, B, note 4, minim–minim. M. 50, CT, note 1, b′. M. 52, note 4–m. 53, note 1, B, minim cum puncto additionis e′–semiminim d′, in minor coloration.

Vat S 51. M. 34, note 3–m. 35, note 3, B, minim cum puncto additionis e–semiminim d–minim c. M. 38, B, notes 3–4, minim b. M. 42, B, note 1, lacks ♭. M. 49, S, note 4, ♭. M. 49, B, note 1, semibrevis–semibrevis. M. 50, CT, note 1, b′. M. 50, note 4–m. 51, note 2, S, minim cum puncto additionis c″–semiminim b–semiminim b–semiminim a. M. 52, note 4–m. 53, note 1, B, minim cum puncto additionis e′–semiminim d′. M. 55, B, note 3, minim–minim. M. 57, S, note 2, fusa g′–fusa f′. M. 59, S, note 2, semibrevis a′–minim g′, in minor coloration. M. 65, S, note 1, semiminim c″–semiminim b′.

VerBC 755. M. 42, B, note 1, lacks ♭. M. 50, CT, note 1, b′. M. 50, note 4–m. 51, note 2, S, minim cum puncto additionis c″–semiminim b–semiminim b–semiminim a. M. 52, note 4–m. 53, note 1, B, semibrevis e′–minim d′, in minor coloration. M. 57, S, note 2, fusa g′–fusa f′. M. 59, S, note 2, minim cum puncto additionis a′–semiminim g′. M. 65, S, note 1, lacking.

VerBC 761. M. 34, note 3–m. 35, note 3, B, minim cum puncto additionis e–semiminim d–minim c. M. 38, B, notes 3–4, minim b. M. 42, B, note 1, lacks ♭. M. 50, CT, note 1, b′. M. 52, note 4–m. 53, note 1, B, semibrevis e′–minim d′, in minor coloration. M. 57, S, note 2, fusa g′–fusa f′. M. 65, S, note 1, semiminim c″–semiminim b′.

Benedictus

JenaU 32. Mm. 67–110, T, 40 brevis rests (44 are required) followed by mensuration sign 3 and four brevis rests (the latter belong to the Osanna). Mm. 67–110, B, 40 brevis rests (44 are required). M. 93, S, note 2, minim g–minim rest. M. 104, S, notes 2–3, minim c″.

Vat S 51. M. 71, CT, note 2, longa. M. 86, note 5–m. 87, note 1, CT, minim cum puncto additionis c′–semiminim d′. M. 87, S, note 2, c″. M. 103, S, note 2, ♭. M. 108, note 4–m. 109, note 1, S, semibrevis d″–minim c″, in minor coloration.

VerBC 755. M. 71, CT, note 3, semiminim b–semiminim a. M. 86, note 5–m. 87, note 1, CT, minim cum puncto additionis c′–semiminim d′. M. 104, S, notes 2–3, minim c″. M. 108, note 4–m. 109, note 1, S, minim cum puncto additionis d″–semiminim c″.

VerBC 761. M. 86, note 5–m. 87, note 1, CT, minim cum puncto additionis c′–semiminim d′. M. 104, S, notes 2–3, minim c″. M. 107, CT, note 2, minim cum puncto additionis d′–semiminim c′. M. 108, note 4–m. 109, note 1, S, minim cum puncto additionis d″–semiminim c″.

Osanna

JenaU 32. M. 118, CT, notes 2–3, imperfect brevis g′. M. 130, S, note 1, imperfect brevis–semibrevis rest. M. 136, note 1–m. 137, note 1, CT, perfect brevis–imperfect brevis. M. 137, T, notes 1–2, perfect brevis. M. 138, B, note 2, lacks ♭. M. 140, CT, g′.

Vat S 51. M. 130, note 1–m. 131, note 1, B, perfect brevis d–brevis a. M. 135, note 1–m. 136, note 1, T, imperfect longa g–semibrevis g′. M. 136, note 1–m. 137, note 1, CT, brevis–semibrevis–brevis.

VerBC 755. M. 116, S, notes 1–3, brevis b′–minim c″–minim d″. M. 123, B, notes 1–2, semibrevis cum puncto additionis d′–minim c′–minim cum additionis c′–semiminim b. M. 130, note 1–m. 131, note 1, B, perfect brevis d–brevis a. M. 135, note 1–m. 136, note 1, T, imperfect longa g–semibrevis g′. M. 136, note 1–m. 137, note 1, CT, brevis–semibrevis–brevis. M. 140, S, note 1, brevis–longa.

VerBC 761. M. 116, S, notes 1–3, brevis b′–minim c″–minim d″. M. 128, S, note 2, ♭. M. 131, rest 1–note 1, B, brevis a. M. 135, note 1–m. 136, note 1, T, imperfect longa g–semibrevis g′. M. 136, note 1–m. 137, note 1, CT, brevis–semibrevis–brevis.

Agnus Dei

ModE M.1.13 lacks the Agnus Dei 2 which is copied into the concordant sources. Instead, the words of Agnus Dei 2 and Agnus Dei 3 are underlaid, in correct sequence, in the second section of music (Agnus Dei 3). The main source for the edition of Agnus Dei 2 is VatS 51.

Agnus Dei 1

JenaU 32. M. 7, T, notes 1–2, semibrevis. M. 9, rest 1–m. 10, note 1, CT, semiminim g–minim d′–minim e′–semiminim f′. M. 9, note 4–m. 10, note 1, T, semiminim g–minim c′–semiminim d′. M. 14, B, notes 1–2, semibrevis. M. 15, T, notes 3–5, minim cum puncto additionis a–semiminim g. M. 16, S, note 3, g′. M. 23, S, note 4, minim cum puncto additionis a′–semiminim g′.

VatS 51. M. 1, T, note 1, minim cum puncto additionis c′–semiminim b. M. 7, CT, note 1, semibrevis c′–minim b, in minor coloration. M. 12, note 3–m. 13, note 1, B, semibrevis–minim. M. 16, S, note 3, g′. M. 19, T, note 5, minim cum puncto additionis c–semiminim B. M. 22, CT, notes 4–5, semibrevis c′. M. 23, S, note 1, minim cum puncto additionis g′–semiminim a′. M. 23, S, note 4, minim cum puncto additionis a′–semiminim g′. M. 27, CT, note 2, fusa d′–fusa c′. M. 28, S, notes 5–6, minim d′. M. 30, S, notes 3–5, minim cum puncto additionis d″–semiminim c″. M. 31, S, note 1, semiminim b′–semiminim g′.

VerBC 755. M. 1, T, note 1, minim cum puncto additionis c′–semiminim b. M. 12, note 3–m. 13, note 1, B, semibrevis–minim. M. 16, S, note 3, g′. M. 18, S, note 2, fusa g′–fusa f′. M. 19, T, note 5, minim cum puncto additionis c–semiminim B.   M. 22, CT, notes 4–5, semibrevis c'.   M. 23, S, note 1, minim cum puncto additionis g'–semiminim a'.   M. 23, S, note 4, minim cum puncto additionis a'–semiminim g'.   M. 27, CT, note 2, fusa d'–fusa c'.

VerBC 761. M. 1, T, note 1, semibrevis c'–minim b, in minor coloration.   M. 7, CT, note 1, semibrevis c'–minim b, in minor coloration.   M. 14, B, notes 1–2, semibrevis.   M. 16, S, note 3, g'.   M. 19, T, note 5, minim cum puncto additionis c–semiminim B.   M. 22, CT, notes 4–5, semibrevis c'.   M. 23, S, note 1, minim cum puncto additionis g'–semiminim a'.   M. 23, S, note 4, minim cum puncto additionis a'–semiminim g'.   M. 27, CT, note 3–m. 28, note 2, S, semibrevis a'.   M. 27, CT, note 2, fusa d'–fusa c'.   M. 28, S, notes 5–6, minim d'.   M. 30, S, notes 3–5, semibrevis d''–minim c'', in minor coloration.

Agnus Dei 2

VerBC 755. M. 62, note 2–m. 64, note 2, CT, minim c'–minim cum puncto additionis e'–semiminim f'–minim g'–minim a'–minim g'–semibrevis e'.   M. 68, S, notes 2–4, semibrevis a'–semiminim g'–semiminim f'.   M. 74, T, note 4, ♭.

VerBC 761. M. 58, CT, note 5, lacking.

Agnus Dei 3

JenaU 32. M. 84, S, note 2, semiminim c'–semiminim b.   M. 90, CT, note 2, e.   M. 100, T, note 2, lacks ♭.   M. 104, note 6–m. 105, note 1, S, minim cum puncto additionis a'–semiminim g'.   M. 109, note 1–m. 110, note 1, B, brevis cum puncto additionis.   M. 120, note 4–m. 121, note 2, S, semibrevis d''.   M. 121, CT, notes 2–3, minim e'.   M. 125, T, notes 1–6, under mensuration sign ¢, semiminim c'–semiminim b–semiminim a–semiminim g–minim cum puncto additionis f–semiminim e.   M. 131, note 4–m. 132, note 4, T, minim e'–minim d'–semibrevis f'–semiminim e'–semiminim d'.   M. 138, note 1–m. 139, note 1, S, longa.   M. 138, note 1–m. 139, note 1, T, longa.   M. 138, note 1–m. 139, note 1, B, longa.

VatS 51. M. 83, note 1–m. 84, note 2, S, minim b–minim b–minim c'–semibrevis d'–semiminim c'–semiminim b.   M. 89, note 4–m. 90, note 1, S, semibrevis a'–minim g', in minor coloration.   M. 89, CT, notes 2–3, minim cum puncto additionis a–semiminim g.   M. 90, CT, note 2, e'.   M. 94, note 2–m. 95, note 1, B, semibrevis–semibrevis.   M. 101, S, rest 1, minim a.   M. 104, note 6–m. 105, note 1, S, minim cum puncto additionis a'–semiminim g'.   M. 109, B, note 1, semibrevis–semibrevis.   M. 121, CT, notes 2–3, minim e'.   M. 129, T, note 2, lacks ♭.   M. 131, note 4–m. 132, note 1, T, minim e'–semiminim f'–semiminim e'.   M. 132, T, note 4, minim cum puncto additionis b–semiminim a.   M. 138, note 1–m. 139, note 1, S, longa.   M. 138, note 1–m. 139, note 1, T, longa.

VerBC 755. M. 84, S, note 2, semiminim c'–semiminim b.   M. 89, note 4–m. 90, note 1, S, minim cum puncto additionis a'–semiminim g'.   M. 89, CT, notes 2–3, minim cum puncto additionis a–semiminim g.   M. 90, CT, note 2, e'.   M. 94, note 2–m. 95, note 1, B, semibrevis–semibrevis.   M. 101, S, rest 1, minim a.   M. 104, note 6–m. 105, note 1, S, minim cum puncto additionis a'–semiminim g'.   M. 109, B, note 1, semibrevis–semibrevis.   M. 121, CT, notes 2–3, minim e'.   M. 129, T, note 2, lacks ♭.   M. 131, note 4–m. 132, note 1, T, minim e'–semiminim f'–semiminim e'.   M. 132, T, note 4, minim cum puncto additionis b–semiminim a.   M. 138, note 1–m. 139, note 1, CT, brevis–longa.   M. 138, note 1–m. 139, note 1, T, longa.

VerBC 761. M. 83, note 1–m. 84, note 2, S, semibrevis b–minim c'–semibrevis d'–semiminim c'–semiminim b.   M. 89, note 4–m. 90, note 1, S, semibrevis a'–minim g', in minor coloration.   M. 89, CT, notes 2–3, minim cum puncto additionis a–semiminim g.   M. 90, CT, note 2, e'.   M. 94, note 2–m. 95, note 1, B, semibrevis–semibrevis.   M. 101, S, rest 1, minim a.   M. 104, note 6–m. 105, note 1, S, minim cum puncto additionis a'–semiminim g'.   M. 109, B, note 1, semibrevis–semibrevis.   M. 121, CT, notes 2–3, minim e'.   M. 129, T, note 2, lacks ♭.   M. 131, note 4–m. 132, note 1, T, minim e'–semiminim f'–semiminim e'.   M. 132, T, note 4, minim cum puncto additionis b–semiminim a.   M. 138, note 1–m. 139, note 1, S, longa.   M. 138, note 1–m. 139, note 1, T, longa.

Missa Nos amis

Edited by Elaine Moohan.

Unique source. ModE M.1.13, no. IV: tenor incipit "Nos amis."

Kyrie

M. 11, CT, note 3, g'.

Gloria

M. 12, CT, note 2, c'.   M. 135, T, note 1, semibrevis.

Credo

M. 151, B, note 1, F.

Appendix

Polyphonic Models

Cela sans plus

RomeC 2856, fols. 153ᵛ–154ᵛ

Colinet de Lanoy/Johannes Martini

Jen- ta bre- gie- ra bel-la de bon reban.

Je- tes mon

289

Der Pfobenschwancz

TrentC 89, fol. 150ᵛ

Barbingant

291

In feuers hitz

BerlPS 40098, no.221

Anonymous

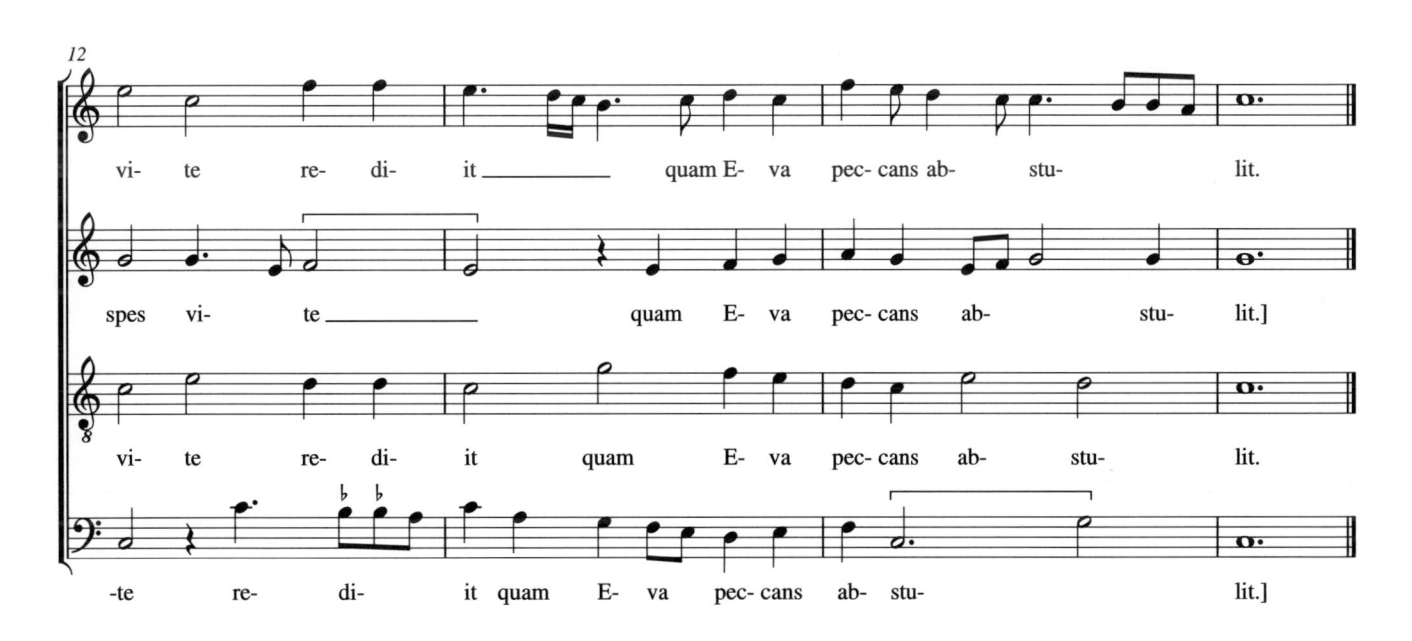

-bis ac-co-mo-da, per quam spes
-rem no-bis ac-co-mo-da, per quam
-bis ac-co-mo-da, per quam spes
-bis ac-co-mo-da, per quam spes vi-

vi-te re-di-it quam E-va pec-cans ab-stu-lit.
spes vi-te quam E-va pec-cans ab-stu-lit.]
vi-te re-di-it quam E-va pec-cans ab-stu-lit.
-te re-di-it quam E-va pec-cans ab-stu-lit.]

La Martinella

RomeC 2856, fols. 54ᵛ–55

Johannes Martini

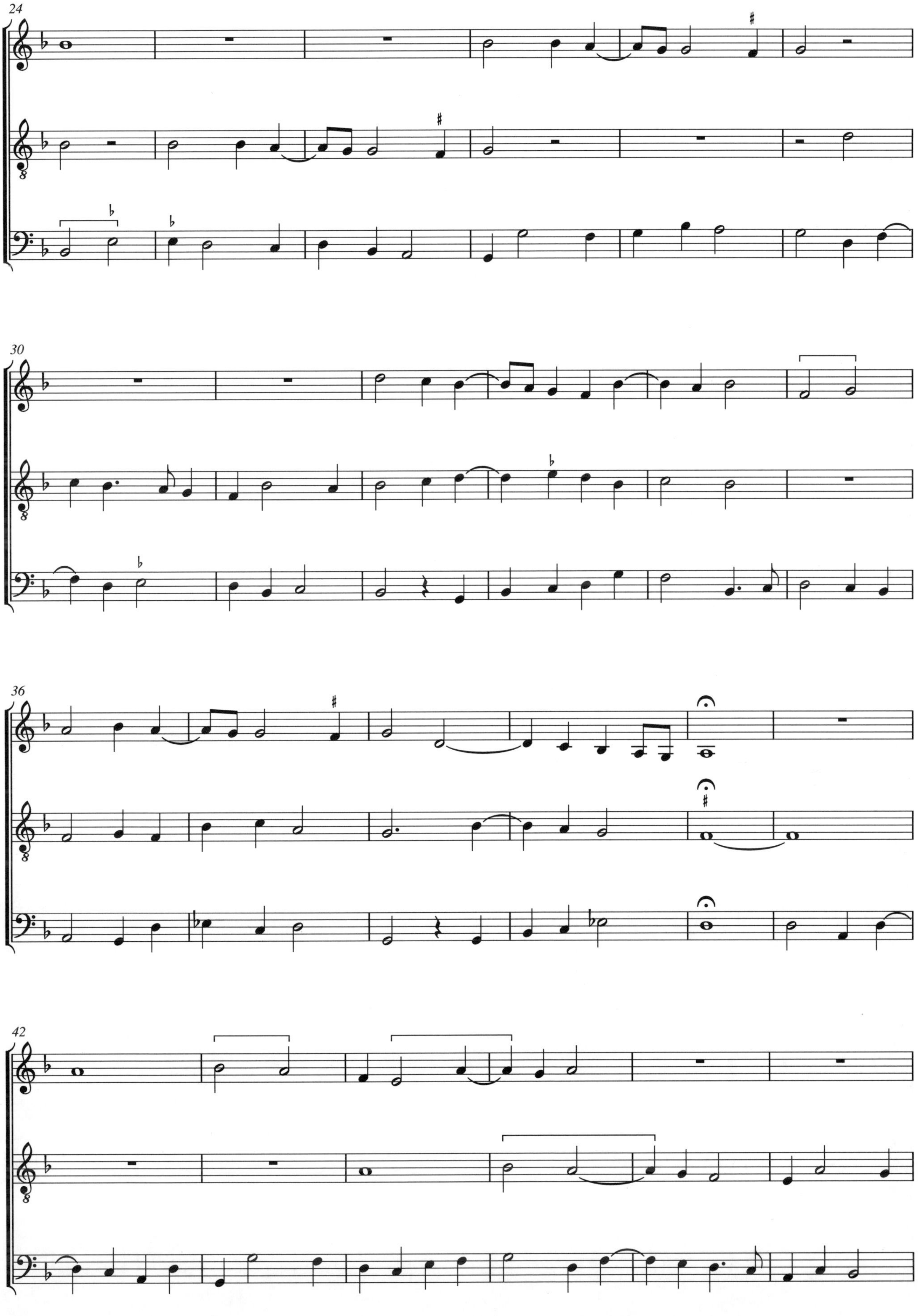
24
30
36
42

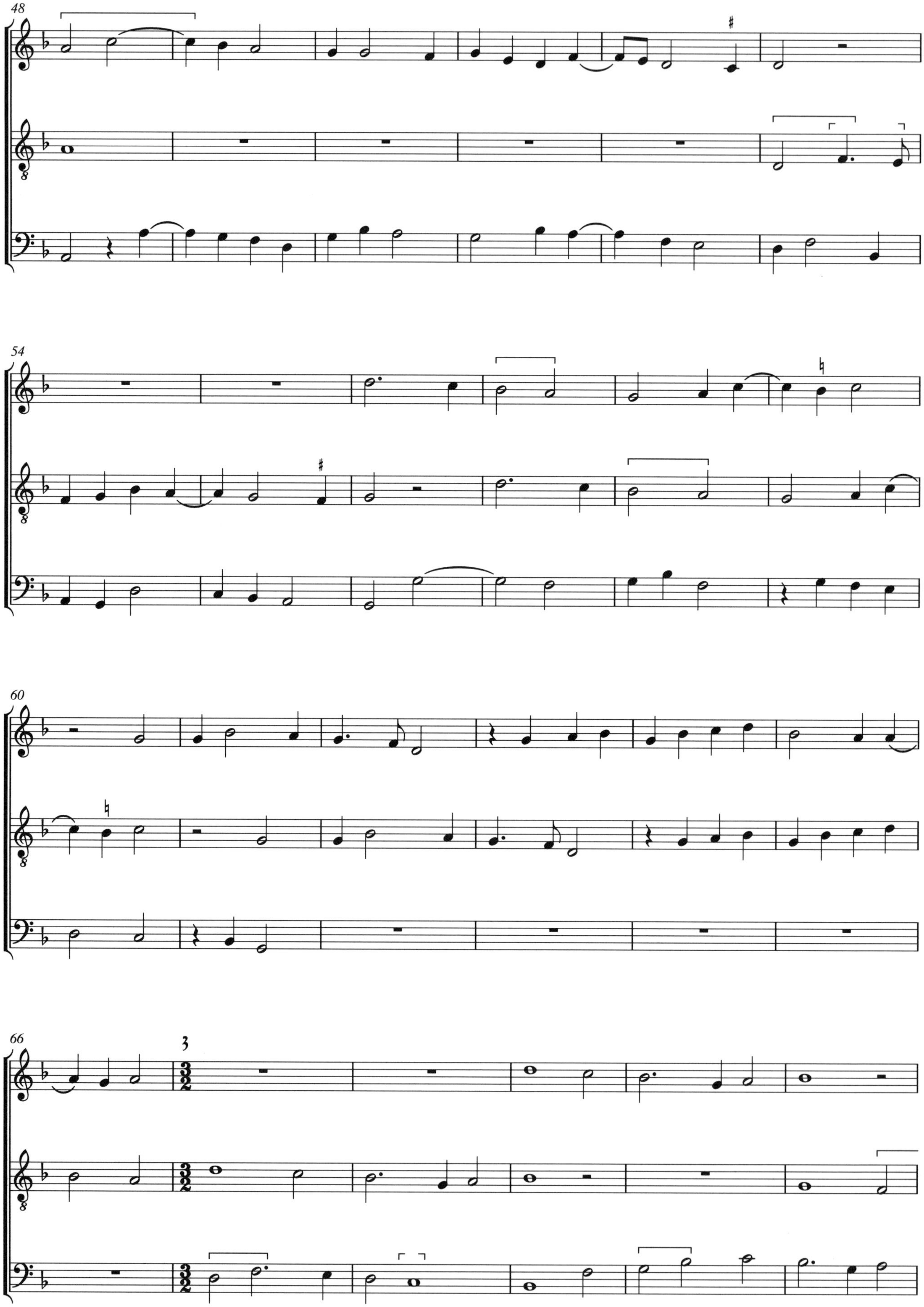
48
54
60
66
3

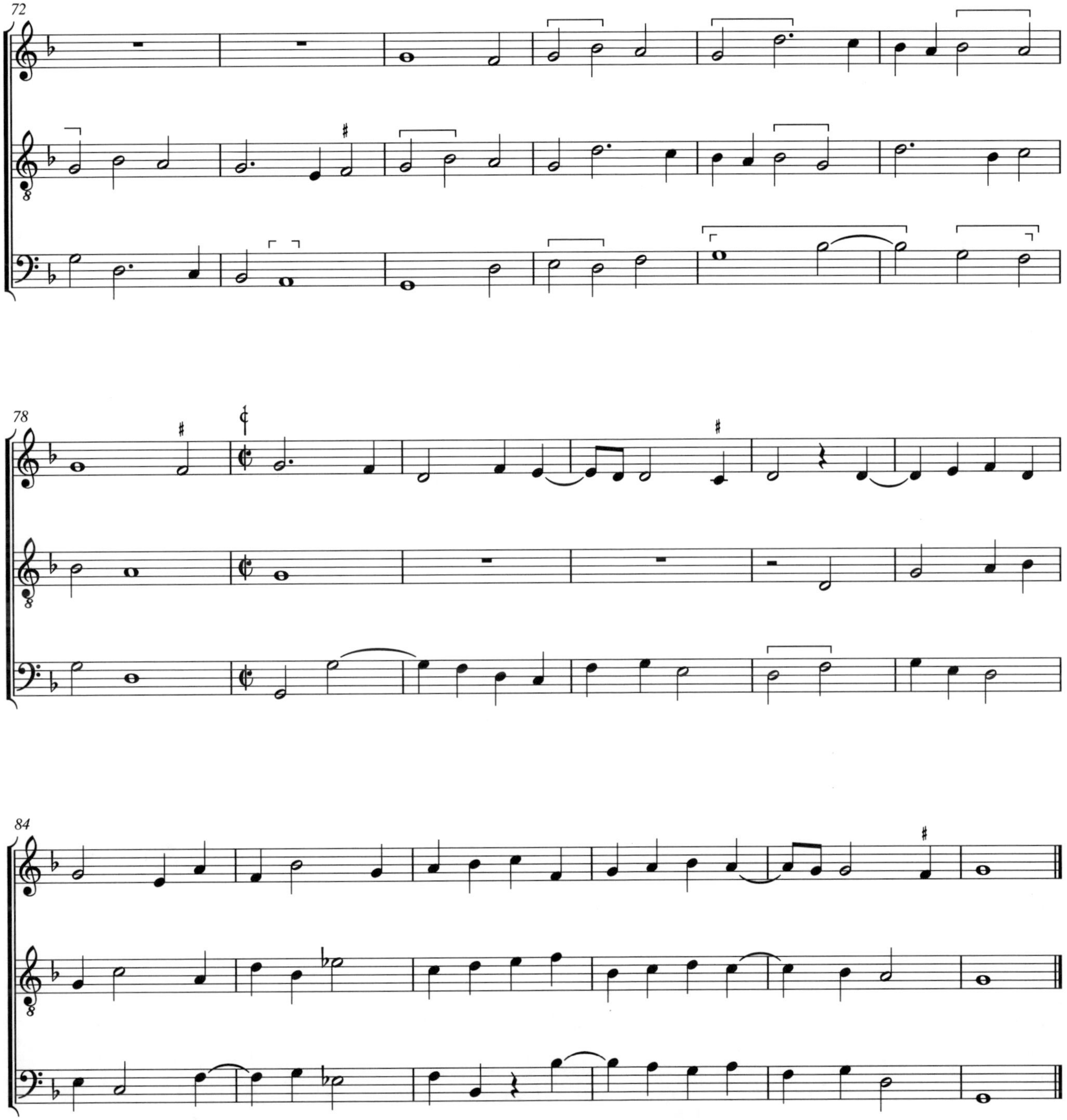
72
78
84

Ma bouche rit

RomeC 2856, fols. 61ᵛ–63

Johannes Okeghem

299

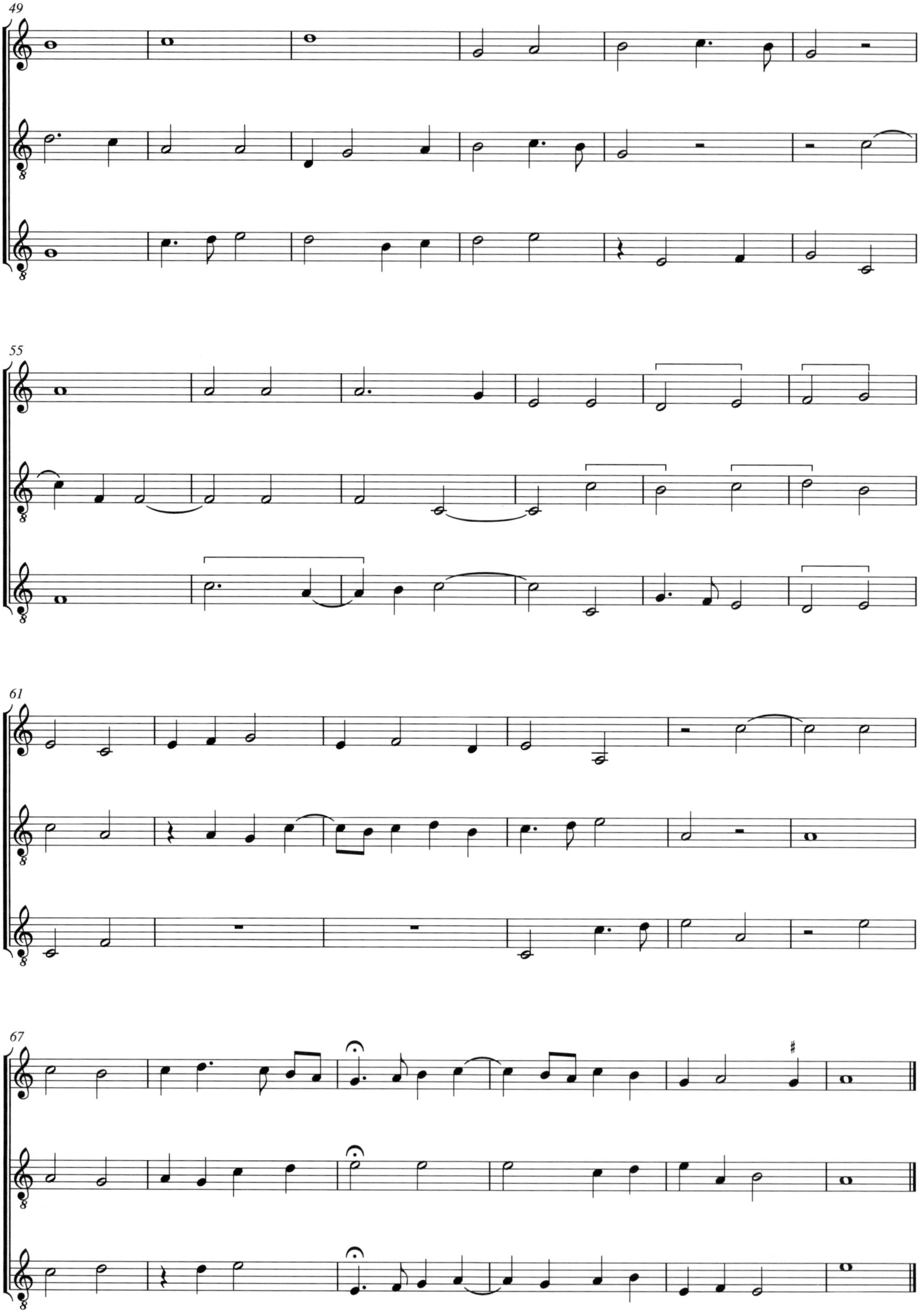
49
55
61
67

Or sus, or sus

PavU 362, fols. 66ᵛ–67

Anonymous

Or sus, or sus! de-par-sus tous les aul-tres be-noit soit le cou-cu! Quar on-que tiel oye-seau ne fut "Je-nin Je-not, es-tu point ma-ri-é?" O-uy beau si-re, que Dieux en ait bon

gré, a u- ne fil- lee qui d'a- mer m'a pri- é.

"Je- nin Je- not! es- tu point ma- ri- é?"

Nos amys

A[drien] Basin

Nos a- mis vous vous a- bu- ses d'at- ten- dre l'a- mou- reu- se gra- ce Aul- tre que vous a prins la pla- ce vos- tre fran- chois en vain u- ses.

Nos a- mys vous vous a- bu- ses

Nos a- mys

Notes and Texts

Missa Cela sans plus

Model. Cela sans plus—Colinet de Lanoy with *si placet* bassus by Johannes Martini.

Primary source. RomeC 2856: headed "Colinet de Lanoy"; tenor incipit "Se la sans plus"; bassus marked "si placet Io Martini."

Concordant sources. See the full list of sources in HewCB.

References. HewCB, p. 137; MartiniS, p. 5.

Missa Coda di Pavon

Model. Der Pfobenschwancz—Barbingant.

Primary source. TrentC 89, fol. 105v: superius headed "O quam clara."

Concordant sources. HradKM 7, p. 389: headed "Berbignant"; tenor incipit "pfobenswancz." BerlPS 40098, no. 208: headed "Der pfawen swancz." MunBS Germ 810, fols. 43v–44: headed "Berbingant Der pfobenswanzc." MunBS Lat 5023, fol. 11v–12: in two voices, text "Da pacem domine." PradP 47, fols. 217–18: text "Ave rosa speciosa."

References. EDM 4, p. 88; CMM 7/2, p. 9.

Missa In feuers hitz

Model. In feuers hitz—Anonymous.

Primary source. BerlPS 40098, no. 221.

Concordant source. MunBS Germ 810, fols. 135v–136.

Changes to the primary source. M. 10, A, note 3, e′, note 4, d′.

References. EDM 4, p. 21; EDM 84, no. 118.

TEXT AND TRANSLATION

Mole gravati criminum,
regina, mater omnium,
ad te currentes poscimus:
adesto nostris precibus.

Eterne vite ianua,
aurem nobis accomoda,
per quam spes vite rediit
quam Eva peccans abstulit.

In feurs hytcz so glut mein hercz,
mein syn und mein gedanken
nach dir, mein lib, mit grossem smerczen
in rechter treu an wancken.

Ich scheid von dir wan es muss sein.
Verschleus mich, lib, in dein schrein.
Das hercze mein sent sich so hart,
Ich freu mich nur der widerfart.

*

Burdened by the weight of crime,
Queen, mother of us all,
hurrying to you we ask:
look favorably on our prayers.

Door of eternal life,
[Mary,] lend us an ear,
Through which the hope of life returns
Which Eve's sinning took away.

My heart, my senses, and my thoughts
are aglow in the passion of fire
for you, my dear; with great pain
they hesitate in proper faithfulness.

I depart from you when I must.
Enshrine me, dear, in your heart.
My heart feels it so deeply
I am glad only when that happens.

Commentary. The model given here carries a Latin contrafactum text. Both the Latin text from the "Glogauer Liederbuch" (BerlPS 40098) and the German text from the "Schedel Liederbuch" (MunBS Germ 810) are shown for comparison.

Missa La Martinella

Model. La Martinella—Johannes Martini.

Primary source. RomeC 2856, fols. 54v–55: headed "Jo. Martini."

Concordant sources. BerlPS 40098, no. 268. BolC Q16, fols. 93v–94. FlorBN BR 229, fols. 12v–13: headed "Jannes Martini." ParisBNF 15123, fols. 145v–146. SegC s.s., fol. 197v–198 (with a different contratenor): headed "Ysaac." SevC 5-1-43, fol. 5v (S and CT only). TrentC 89, fols. 389v–390 (textless): headed "Johannes Martini." TrentC 91, fols. 257v–258. VatG XIII.27, fols. 29v–30: headed "Johannes Martini." VerBC 757, fols. 17v–18. WarU 2016, fols. 113v–114. 1538[9], no. 36. BasU F.IX.22, fols. 27v–30 (keyboard intabulation): headed "Isacio."

References. BrowFC, no. 13; DTÖ 14–15, p. 223; DTÖ 28, p. 150; EDM 4, p. 62; MartiniS, pp. 47–49; MarxT, p. 26.

Missa Ma bouche rit

Model. Ma bouche rit—Johannes Okeghem.

Primary source. RomeC 2856, fols. 61v–63 (51v–53), Okeghem.

Concordant sources. BerlPS 40098, no. 267. CopKB 1848, p. 401. DijM 517, fols. iv′–vi. FlorBN Mag.176, fols. 32v–34: headed "Ocheghem." FlorR 2356, fols. 28v–29 (34v–35). MunBS Germ 810, fols. 62v–64: headed "Ockegheim." NHavY 91, fols. 38v–40: headed "Okeghem." ParisBN 57, fols. lii′–liv: headed "Okeghem." ParisBNF 15123, fols. 30v–32. ParisBNN 4379, fols. 4v–6 (e5v–e7). ParisBNR 2973, fols. 42v–43. VatG XIII.27, fols. 76v–77 (69v–70). WashLC L25, fols. 32v–34. WolfA 287, fols. 29v–31. 1501, fols. 59v–60: headed "Okenhem." 1538[9], no. 86.

References. AMMM 12, pp. 29–31; DrozT, no. 5; EDM 4, no. 267; EitWL, suppl., no. 8; GomO, Notenanhang, no. 5; HAM 1, no. 75; HewO, no. 54; OckW 3, pp. 73–74; PerkMC, no. 30; WolfS, no. 14.

Missa Or sus, or sus

Model. Orsus, orsus—Anonymous.
Unique source. PavU 362, fols. 66v–67: full text in tenor.
Concordant source. None.
References. None.
Changes to the primary source. M. 18, CT, note 1, g. M. 24, CT, note 2, e'. Text line seven has "Veniz" in place of "Jenin."

Text and Translation

Or sus, or sus! deparssus tous les aultres
benoit soit le coucu!
Quar onque tiel oyeseau ne fut.
"Jenin Jenot, es-tu point marié?"
"Ouy, beau sire, que Dieux en ait bon gré
a une fille que d'amer m'a prié"
"Jenin Jenot, es-tu point marié?"

*

Come away, come away! above all others
blessed be the cuckoo!
Never was a bird like this seen.
"Jenin Jenot, are you not married?"
"Yes, he says, if it please God,
To a lady who begged me to love her."
"Jenon Jenot, are you not married?"
(translated by A. J. Kennedy and P. Davies)

Missa Nos amis

Model. Nos amys—A[drien] Basin.
Primary source. NHavY 91, fols. 79v–80: headed "A Basin"; full text in superius, incipits in tenor and contratenor.
Concordant source. EscSL IV.a.24, fols. 124v–125.
References. PerkMC, no. 56, p. 13; HanenC, p. 429.